Yahweh and Son

Yahweh and Son

A Teenager's Guide to the Bible

Anthony J. Marinelli

Paulist Press *New York/Mahwah*

BS600.2
M34

Acknowledgments
The Publisher gratefully acknowledges use of the following materials:

"The Road Not Taken" from THE POETRY OF ROBERT FROST, edited by Edward Connery Lathem. Copyright 1916, © 1969 by Holt, Rinehart and Winston. Copyright 1944 by Robert Frost. Reprinted by permission of Holt, Rinehart and Winston, Publishers.

Excerpts from THE JERUSALEM BIBLE, copyright © 1966 by Darton Longman & Todd, Ltd. and Doubleday & Company, Inc. Used by permission of the publisher.

Library of Congress
Catalog Card Number: 85-61744

ISBN: 0-8091-9568-2

Published by Paulist Press
997 Macarthur Boulevard
Mahwah, New Jersey 07430

Printed and bound in the
United States of America

Contents

Introduction

The Bible. Presidents quote from it, and witnesses swear on it in court. It sits in millions of homes throughout our country. Sometimes it is read; at other times it is a useful paperweight—the heaviest book in the house. In some homes, it simply collects dust. It remains the number one best seller in the world. It exists in countless languages and in various translations in the same language. Parents and teachers use it to keep children in line. It is read by preachers promising salvation. It is so versatile that it is said that even the devil himself can quote it for his own purposes. Some versions contain books that others leave out. It is known as the good book, the word of God and the Scriptures. In it there are some of the most famous stories in the world. It is not only concerned with religion; there are also tales of love and betrayal, war, politics and sex. There are endless rules and regulations concerning everything from worshiping God to the mating of cattle.

Yet as difficult and obscure as it can be, men and women still look to it in times of prayer and in need of inspiration. It is at these times that we are able to see the Bible's true meaning and purpose: its words are meant to speak to our hearts and minds, giving us faith and hope, inspiring us to love and care, moving us more deeply into the mystery of God's love and will for us. This book is written as an encouragement to reading and understanding the Bible and discovering the unique way in which God offers himself to each of us. Because this book is written from a Christian perspective, it will focus on the New Testament and more specifically on the person of Jesus as the fulfillment of God's revelation.

1

A Few Helpful Hints for Reading the Bible

1. It's the Latest, It's the Greatest, It's a Library

One of most important things to remember when reading the Bible is that it is not a book. It is many books. In fact, it is much more like a library than a single book. Some of the books were formulated a thousand years after others had already taken shape. And just like any library, there are many different types of books. There are stories, fables, sayings, poetry, history, books of law, gospels, letters and more. These different types are called "literary forms." When reading from the Bible, it is very important to be aware of the literary form we are dealing with. If we were reading a religious story and thought that it was historically true we might miss the whole point of the story. For example, the Book of Job in the Bible is a story about the mystery of suffering and evil in the world. In the story, God does all kinds of terrible things to Job including killing his family, servants and animals. If we were to read this as a factually true story, we would certainly not want any part of this religious tradition and we would miss the real meaning of the story.

2. The Bible Is Inspired by God But Written by Men

It is our custom to call the Bible the word of God and to say that God is the author of the Bible. This is true but only if we understand it correctly. God is considered the author of the Bible because we believe that he was the inspiration behind it. However, the books of the Bible were written by people. This fact raises some important questions. Did the writers of the Bible know they were writing the inspired word of God? Did they have some special arrangement with God? Did God dictate these words to the authors? No, this is not what is meant by inspiration. How then is the Bible inspired? It is said to be inspired because the authors accurately reflect the faith of Israel and Christianity. The authors and editors used their own faith, wisdom and decisions in writing and compiling the stories. However, we believe that in the midst of this very human process was the inspiring presence of God. Maybe a brief story can help shed a little light on the subject.

I remember leaving the house several winters ago on a freezing evening in New York to go to the movies. When I was getting ready to go, I noticed that there were two winter coats in my closet—my "old" one and a recent Christmas present. Just on a hunch I brought both coats with me. Walking to my car from the theater with the temperature less than ten degrees, I saw a man huddled near the side of the building trying to protect himself from the cold wind. All he owned was a light windbreaker. He was also the answer to my hunch, and I gave him the extra coat. I'm sure, in a sense, that the hunch was inspired by God, but I certainly heard no voices. The "inspiration" did come from a faith that has always taught me that "whatsoever you do for the least of my brothers, you do for me" (Mt 25:40). Similarly, when the authors of the Bible reflect the truth of their faith in Yahweh and in Jesus, they do it only under the inspiration of God who uses their faith and intelligence to communicate.

3. Not All Books Are Created Equal

If the Bible is the true revelation of God's plan of salvation, not all of it is equally revealing. Some books are much more important than others. For Christians, the New Testament is more important than the Old Testament, and in the New Testament the Gospels are more important than anything else. Because the Bible is so large this is an important point to remember if you decide to read certain parts. If you are reading the Bible for spiritual insight or to pray, don't think that you can just open the Bible anywhere and God will speak to you. This can be a lot more frustrating than helpful. Later on in the book I will offer some suggestions on how to read the Bible for prayer and meditation.

4. Fundamentalism and the Bible

There are many people who interpret the Bible literally. This means that they believe that every word in the Bible is true as written. They give little or no consideration to the literary form or to the cultural background of the authors. This interpretation of the Bible is known as fundamentalism. A fundamentalist would insist that the world was created in six days because the Bible says so, despite the fact that the scientific evidence does not support their position. Although Catholics may have several things in common with some fundamentalist groups—faith in Jesus, commitment to the poor—our interpretation of the Bible is different. The Catholic Church does not interpret the entire Bible literally and believes that to do so runs the risk of distorting the true meaning of the Bible.

1

The Discovery of Yahweh

We mentioned in the Introduction that the Bible is not a single book as much as it is a collection of books. Since we will spend only a brief amount of time and space examining the Old Testament, how can we possibly do justice to all forty-six books? Obviously, we cannot. What shall we choose to focus on in the Old Testament? Is it possible to find a thread that connects all these diverse books? Perhaps there is. John L. McKenzie, one of the great Scripture scholars of our time, believes that there is. What is this thread?

> It can only be the discovery of Yahweh, the God of Israel. . . . The discovery of Yahweh was something like the discovery of America; it took several centuries before Israel really began to realize what it had discovered. Yet Yahweh is a single reality.

Israel's understanding of their God was something that grew and developed in time. The Old Testament is the story of a people being called by their God into a deeper relationship with him. It brings together the different insights of the great religious figures of Judaism: Moses, David, the prophets and others. We would like to show some of the important breakthroughs that Israel experienced in understanding their God and examine whether their

insights have any relevance for us today in our own journey of
faith.

Yahweh

Names are interesting. Often you can tell something about
people's ancestry by their name. Johnson probably started off as
John's son. The Smiths of the world may find a village blacksmith
or silversmith in their past. When we want to know people, the
first thing we ask is their names. Our name gives us a distinctive
identity.

The same held true for the Israelites and their relationship
with God. God's name was not simply a way of referring to God.
God's name was sacred and revealed the very nature of God.
When Moses encounters God in the burning bush, he asks his
name. This doesn't seem like a strange request. But the answer
that God gives Moses certainly seems like a strange answer:

> Then Moses said to God, "I am to go then to the sons of Israel
> and say to them, 'The God of your fathers has sent me to
> you.' But if they ask me what his name is, what am I to tell
> them?" And God said to Moses, "I Am who I Am. This is
> what you must say to the sons of Israel: I AM has sent me to
> you" (Ex 3:13–14).

I Am? What sort of a strange name is this, and what could
possibly be meant by it? Would not God have been a lot clearer
if he had said "I am the Powerful One" or "I am the Creator"?
Why "I Am who I Am" (in Hebrew, this translates into Yahweh)? In fact, this name Yahweh is telling us something very important about the God of Israel. Yahweh is the one who *is*. People
come and go, plants and flowers come and go, nations and civi-
lizations come and go, but Yahweh *is*. Yahweh is infinitely

greater than man or creation. He *is* eternal. Sometimes when we think about God being eternal we imagine that he will go on forever, and this is true. However, there is more to it than that. The name Yahweh implies absolutely no limits to God. Because he is eternal he is able to be present to every man, woman and child in every age and nation. Because he is eternal there are no limits to the ways in which he is able to be present to us. He is present as Father, Mother, Friend. He is male and female. He is compassionate, warm, and loving. He is challenging, firm, demanding. The God that Moses experienced in the burning bush was I AM, Yahweh, the God without limits.

Moses is certainly not the only human being to experience God's presence. What he experienced in the burning bush, others have experienced in different ways. It is the experience of God's infinite greatness.

Many years ago I remember going to Long Beach on Long Island in the early evening and watching the sun go down from a deserted shoreline. I climbed out on the rocks of the jetty and simply took in the beauty as the waves crashed on the beach. It occurred to me that the same ocean had been rushing to the shore for thousands of years. The stars that shone above me had existed for millions of years. There had never been a wave or a star that God was not always aware of. Yahweh—the God without limits. No great voice from a burning bush, but perhaps what I felt that night was a tiny bit of what Moses felt three thousand years ago in the presence of Yahweh.

In the Bible there are many references to the greatness of Yahweh and his all-powerful, all-knowing nature. None of them is more beautiful than Psalm 139:

> Yahweh, you examine me and know me;
> you know if I am standing or sitting.
> You read my thoughts from far away,

whether I walk or lie down, you are watching;
you know every detail of my conduct.

The word is not even on my tongue,
Yahweh, before you know all about it;
close behind and close in front you fence me round
shielding me with your hand.
Such knowledge is beyond my understanding,
a height to which my mind cannot attain.

Where could I go to escape your spirit?
Where could I flee from your presence?
If I climb to the heavens you are there,
there, too, if I lie in Sheol.

If I flew to the point of sunrise,
or westward across the sea,
your hand would still be guiding me,
your right hand holding me.

If I asked the darkness to cover me,
and light to become night around me,
that darkness would not be dark to you,
night would be as light as day.

It was you who created my inmost self,
and put me together in my mother's womb:
for all these mysteries I thank you:
for the wonder of myself, for the wonder of your works.

For Personal Reflection

Moses experienced the presence of God in the burning bush.
To Moses, God revealed himself as I AM. Has there ever been a
time in your life when you felt that God was somehow mysteriously present? I doubt that you have seen a burning bush, but per-

haps the experience had to do with nature, or love, the experience of death or suffering, or the reception of a sacrament. Take some time to describe the experience on paper. What were you feeling about yourself and God? How would you describe God from this experience?

The Many Faces of Yahweh

Have you ever noticed that each of us is really many different people? Depending on whom you ask, I am either a son or a husband, a teacher, a brother or a friend. My wife, mother, friends, brothers, sister and students all see the same person, yet they all see slightly different aspects of me. When asked to describe me, their descriptions would have many things in common, yet there would also be differences. If they were asked five years ago, the responses would have been different, and fifteen years ago they would have been very different. A person's relationship with us will affect the way that person tends to see us.

The same holds true for Yahweh and his relationship with the Israelites. Depending on the time, people and circumstances, Yahweh revealed himself in many different ways. The God that Moses discovered in the burning bush had only just begun a long, adventuresome relationship with the Jewish people. Christians believe that the climax of God's revealing of himself finally occurred in person—the person of Jesus. But for now, let's take a look at four different ways in which Yahweh revealed himself to his people.

1. Yahweh, the Savior

The time: about 1200 B.C.

The place: Egypt, the Sea of Reeds

The scene: The Hebrew people have been the slaves of the Egyptian Pharaoh, Ramses II. The Israelite Moses is given a special mission by God: he is to lead his people out of slavery and oppression. After a series of plagues, Pharaoh allows the Israelites to leave, but he changes his mind at the last minute and chases the Hebrews with chariots. At the Sea of Reeds the Israelites escape while the chariots of Pharaoh are trapped by the sea. Against incredible odds this band of slaves have escaped from the power of the mighty Egyptian army. The Israelites bestow their praise on Yahweh for saving them from Pharaoh and freeing them from slavery. In Exodus 15 we find a "folk song" that was sung by the Jews for hundreds of years to recall Yahweh's saving power:

> Yahweh I sing: he has covered himself in glory,
> horse and rider he has thrown into the sea.
> Yahweh is my strength, my song,
> he is my salvation.
> This is my God, I praise him,
> the God of my father I extol him.
> Yahweh is a warrior;
> Yahweh is his name.
> The chariots and army of Pharaoh
> he has hurled into the sea;
> the pick of his horsemen
> lie drowned in the Sea of Reeds.
> The depths have closed over them;
> they have sunk to the bottom like a stone (Ex 15:1–5).

In this song, Yahweh is described as a warrior who powerfully leads his people into battle. This is hardly an image that we would use today in the Church to describe God. But these are primitive people. They believe that Yahweh wants them to be free from slavery, and war seemed the only way to freedom—so Yahweh was the great warrior.

Another important question has been raised about this story. Did it actually happen the way it is described in the fourteenth chapter of Exodus with the sea dividing in two and the Israelites marching through, and the sea then uniting again to drown the on-coming army of Pharaoh? The answer is that we are not sure how the event took place. However, there are a lot of good reasons to doubt this version of the story. To begin with, the account of the story in Exodus 14 is really two accounts joined together. The more famous account has already been mentioned, but if you look carefully you will be able to find the traces of a different rendition:

> Yahweh drove back the sea with a strong easterly wind all night and he made dry land of the sea. . . . In the morning watch, Yahweh looked down on the army of the Egyptians . . . and threw the army into confusion. He so clogged their chariot wheels that they could scarcely make headway (Ex 14:21–25).

The stories that we find written in the Bible were usually passed down for hundreds of years by word of mouth. This story was written hundreds of years after the actual event and seems to have taken on two variations. This second version is less spectac-ular. It speaks of the wind drying up the edge of the sea and the chariots being unable to operate on such soft ground. There is, however, an important point that both stories agree on very much: the escape from slavery and Egypt was much more than the work of Moses—it was the work of Yahweh himself. It was Yahweh who had saved his people.

For Personal Reflection

What does it mean for you to believe that God is your Savior?

What does he save you from?

2. Yahweh, the Lawgiver

Did you ever play a game in which the rules were not clear
or were being changed as the game went along? It's not much fun.
We need rules in games to insure order and fairness. The same is
true with the society that we live in. The laws of a society are
generally meant to protect the rights and values of individuals and
the community. For example, we have laws against speeding in
order to ensure people's safety. Good laws help us to do what is
best for ourselves and others. In this sense, the Israelites saw Yahweh as the ultimate lawgiver. God desires that the people he has
freed from slavery care for and respect one another. Of course,
the most famous group of laws associated with Yahweh and the
Israelites is the Ten Commandments:

> Then God spoke all these words. He said, "I am Yahweh
> your God who brought you out of the land of Egypt, out of
> the house of slavery.
> You shall have no other gods except me.
> You shall not make yourself a carved image or any likeness
> of anything in heaven or on earth beneath or in the waters
> beneath the earth: you shall not bow down to them or serve
> them. For I, Yahweh, am a jealous God and I punish the fa-
> ther's fault in the sons, the grandsons and the great grandsons
> of those who hate me; but I show kindness to thousands of
> those who love and keep my commandments.
> You shall not utter the name of Yahweh your God to misuse,
> for Yahweh will not leave unpunished the man who utters his
> name to misuse it.
> Remember the sabbath day and keep it holy. For six days you
> shall labor and do all your work, but the seventh is a sabbath
> for Yahweh your God. . . .
> Honor your father and your mother so that you might have a
> long life in the land that Yahweh your God has given you.
> You shall not kill.

You shall not commit adultery.
You shall not steal.
You shall not bear false witness against your neighbor.
You shall not covet your neighbor's house. You shall not covet your neighbor's wife or his servant, man or woman, or his ox or his donkey or anything that is his (Ex 20:1–17).

These Commandments represent the highpoint of the law of Yahweh. For their time and culture, they represent a very high level of moral behavior. However, the Jewish law also always reflected the time and culture that the people lived in. If you continue reading beyond the Ten Commandments (Ex 20–23), you will see that Yahweh gave many other laws. One of these laws states, "If a man beats his slave, male or female, and the slave dies at his hands, he must pay the penalty. But should the slave survive for one or two days, he shall pay no penalty because the slave is his by right of purchase." It sounds as if Yahweh is in favor of slavery and is uncaring about the rights of the slave. The Bible says this is God's law, but it sounds unfair to us.

How can we solve this problem? Is God unfair and uncaring? Of course not. The problem comes about because we misunderstand the way that the Bible was written. The Bible was written by men and inspired by God. Because it is written by humans, and in this case somewhat primitive humans, *it reflects their understanding of God's will and law.* When you read the Ten Commandments you can see that there is a great deal of wisdom in them—wisdom that remains true three thousand years later. However, the Commandments and the other laws of Yahweh reflect not only the wisdom and inspiration of God, but the limitations of the biblical authors.

It would be unwise to become preoccupied with the limitations of the authors of the Bible and miss the truly important point here: it is by obedience to the law of Yahweh that the Israelite achieves his salvation. The person who followed the law of Yahweh would prosper and know happiness, but the sinner would be lost. This wisdom that the Israelites had discovered is beautifully expressed in Psalm 1:

> Happy the man who follows not the counsel of the wicked
> nor walks in the way of the sinners,
> nor sits in the company of the insolent,
> but delights in the law of the Lord
> and meditates on his law day and night.
> He is like a tree planted near running water,
> that yields its fruit in due season,
> and whose leaves never fade.
> (Whatever he does prospers.)
>
> Not so the wicked, not so;
> they are like chaff which the wind blows away.
> Therefore in judgment the wicked shall not stand
> nor shall the sinners in the assembly of the just.
> For the Lord watches over the way of the just,
> but the way of the wicked vanishes.

What can we conclude from this? If we are obedient to the law of God will we attain salvation? Well, yes and no. Obedience to the law of God is very important, but it may not be enough. Let's face it—if all God wanted was obedience, he could have stopped creating after he made the dog. They seem easier to train than human beings. But the purpose of God's law goes deeper than simple obedience. The purpose of God's law is that we may love him more deeply. Deeper than our obedience, God desires our hearts. In the Old Testament it was the prophet Jeremiah who made this point clear:

> See, the days are coming—it is Yahweh who speaks—when
> I will make a new covenant with the house of Israel (and the

house of Judah), but not a covenant like the one I made with their ancestors when I took them by the hand and led them out of the land of Egypt. They broke that covenant of mine, so I had to show them who was master. It is Yahweh who speaks. No, this is the covenant I will make with the House of Israel when those days arrive—it is Yahweh who speaks. *Deep within them I will plant my law writing it in their hearts.* Then I shall be their God and they shall be my people (Jer 31:31–33).

Through the escape from Egypt and the Ten Commandments, Yahweh had entered into a special relationship with the Israelites. This relationship was known as a covenant. The terms of the covenant were the Commandments which the Israelites were to obey. However, Jeremiah looks to the day when this relationship shall not be as much a matter of obedience but of love. There will be a new covenant; however, it will not be written on stone tablets, but in their hearts. Later on Jesus will identify himself with the new covenant of Jeremiah. "This is the new covenant in my blood which is to be shed for you" (Lk 22:20).

For Personal Reflection

1. If Yahweh were to deliver ten commandments for the United States, what do you think they should be?

2. "The purpose of God's law goes deeper than simple obedience. The purpose of God's law is that we may love him more deeply." How does the law help us to love God? What's the difference between "simple obedience" and love?

3. Yahweh, a God of Compassion and Justice

Moses had come down from Mount Sinai and delivered the Commandments to the Israelites. After the last Commandment is listed, the Book of Exodus then says, *"All the people shook with fear* at the peals of thunder and the lightning flashes, and the sound of trumpets and the smoking mountain, *and they kept their distance:* . . . Moses answered the people, 'Do not be afraid; God has come to test you, so that your fear of him, being always in your mind, may keep you from sinning' " (Ex 20:18–20).

What is the first reaction of the Israelites to Yahweh the Lawgiver? It is one of fear. Moses confirms that Yahweh has put this fear into them so that they will not sin. If we understand God only in terms of being a lawgiver, then he is someone to be feared. God makes the laws and punishes those who break them. This can be a very tough God to live with. We always have to be on our toes, making sure that everything that we do is perfect, because God is always watching for any slip-ups. This seems to be the idea that some of the people in the Old Testament had about God. In fact many people today only see God as Lawgiver. I remember being told as a child that God watches over us and writes down everything that we do in a book, and that when we die, he weighs the good against the bad and decides whether we go to heaven or hell. There is a grain of truth in this: God is always present to us, and much of our judgment will depend on how we lived our lives. However, there is also a big problem with this type of thinking. God seems only to be a God of justice (like a judge) and not a God of mercy. But, in time, Israel began to emphasize the mercy of Yahweh as well as his justice. This realization comes through in the Psalms and especially in the prophets.

We are not really sure who wrote all of the Psalms. Many of them were ascribed to the great king, David. Tradition has it that David wrote Psalm 51 when he had been confronted by Nathan about his unlawful sexual relationship with Bathsheba. David had committed a terrible sin. He had had sexual relations with Bathsheba, the wife of Uriah. But that was the least of his sin. So that he could take Bathsheba as his own wife, David had also stationed

Uriah at the front of the battle line where he was easily killed.
When confronted by Nathan, Daniel repents of his sin:

> Have mercy on me, O God, in your goodness,
> in your great tenderness wipe away my faults;
> wash me clean of my guilt,
> purify me from my sin.
>
> For I am well aware of my faults.
> I have my sin constantly in mind,
> having sinned against none other than you,
> having done what you regard as wrong.
>
> You are just when you pass sentence on me,
> blameless when you give judgment.
> You know I was born guilty,
> a sinner from the moment of my conception.
>
> Yet since you love sincerity of heart,
> teach me the secrets of wisdom.
> Purify me with the hyssop until I am clean,
> wash me until I am whiter than snow.
>
> Instill some joy and gladness in me,
> let the bones you have crushed rejoice again.
> Hide your face from my sins,
> wipe out all my guilt.
>
> God, create a clean heart in me,
> put into me a new and constant spirit:
> do not banish me from your presence,
> do not deprive me of your holy spirit (Ps 51).

David has been forced to go beyond the simple notion of
Yahweh as Lawgiver-Judge. He needs mercy and he needs for-

giveness. He refers to the tenderness of Yahweh and implores his forgiveness. Yahweh is still the Lawgiver, but he is more. He is the God who offers mercy and a new beginning.

In the Old Testament, it is probably the prophets who show the greatest insight into the compassion of God. For the prophets, the compassion of Yahweh takes basically two forms. First, Yahweh seems to identify himself with the oppressed, the poor and the outcast; second, Yahweh's love remains unconditional in the face of the infidelity and sinfulness of his people.

Perhaps no other prophet is as forceful as Amos in conveying Yahweh's compassion for the oppressed. Amos condemned a phony religious attitude that makes sacrifices to Yahweh but ignores the needs of the poor. The Israelites had developed many rituals to worship Yahweh. These rituals included the sacrifices of animals and the chanting of songs at the feasts. Unfortunately, at the time of Amos (about 750 B.C.) there was a big gap between rich and poor, and many of the rich cared much more about their sacrifices to Yahweh than they did about the poor. Amos speaks on behalf of Yahweh:

> I hate and despise your feasts,
> I take no pleasure in your solemn festivals. . . .
> But if you would offer me holocausts,
> then let justice flow like water,
> and integrity like an unfailing stream (Am 5:21, 24).

> Listen to this, you who trample on the needy
> and try to suppress the poor people of the country (Am 8:4).

Yahweh's heart is with the needy and the poor. He challenges the rich and the fat to change their ways and repent or there will be tragic consequences.

In fact, the people do not repent and before long they experience the most traumatic event in their history. They are defeated by the Babylonians who take the Jews out of their homeland and put them in exile. This event, known as the exile or the Babylonian captivity, was a crushing defeat for the Jews. The land that had been given them by Yahweh was no longer their home. God had abandoned his promise to them. It is difficult for us to imagine the effects of this experience. It was a feeling of guilt and hopelessness. Again the Jews were forced to expand their understanding of Yahweh. Could it be possible that the God of Israel had not abandoned his people? Could it be that he would travel with them to Babylonia and forgive them for their great sins against him?

It is exactly this message that the prophet Isaiah delivers to God's people:

> Console my people, console them, says your God.
> Speak to the heart of Jerusalem and call to her
> that her time of service is ended,
> that her sin is atoned for (Is 40:1–2).

> Here is the Lord coming with power. . . .
> He is like a shepherd feeding his flock,
> gathering lambs in his arms,
> holding them against his breast
> and leading the mother ewes to their rest (Is 40:10–11).

For Isaiah, Yahweh is a God of consolation. He is the shepherd who provides for his flock and gathers the lambs in his arms. Finally Isaiah gives us one of the most beautiful images in the Bible to describe the compassion of God. Yahweh's love for his people is like a mother's love for the child within her womb—and even more:

> For Zion was saying, "Yahweh has abandoned me,
> the Lord has forgotten me."
> Does a woman forget her baby at the breast,
> or fail to cherish the son of her womb?

Yet even if these forget,
I will never forget you (Is 49:14–15).

For Personal Reflection

1. Who are the oppressed in our country today? Who are the prophets today who put themselves on the side of the poor and oppressed?

2. We have been referring to God as "him" throughout these pages. In fact, God is neither male nor female, but has both masculine and feminine characteristics. Isaiah compares Yahweh to a pregnant woman and a nurturing mother. In what way is God's love feminine? Do you ever think of God's love as a mother's love?

Yahweh's Life-Giving Spirit

In the beginning God created the heavens and the earth. Now the earth was a formless void, there was darkness over the deep, and God's spirit (*ruah*) hovered over the water (Gen 1:1–2).

Ruah is a Hebrew word. It is pronounced roo-achh, and it means either wind or breath or spirit.

What does *ruah* have to do with the Israelite understanding of Yahweh? They certainly never called Yahweh "ruah" but they did recognize that an important characteristic of Yahweh was his ability to mysteriously, invisibly act with creative power. That is why *ruah* appears in the story of creation. Yahweh creates miraculously from nothing. *Ruah* is a good word to describe Yahweh's spirit and power, for *ruah* also means wind. We never actually see the wind. What we see are the effects of the wind. During a storm we are able to see the dramatic effects of the wind as branches break, trees bend and people take shelter from its power. Yet the wind remains invisible. We only know of its presence because of its effects.

The same is true with Yahweh. We can see his effects in creation and in ourselves. Whenever the *ruah* of Yahweh is present there is new life, often against great odds. The new life that Yahweh brings is rarely biological life. Rather the *ruah* of Yahweh often brings hope to the despairing, love to the lonely and joy to the brokenhearted. One of the great testimonies of the ruah of Yahweh is given by the prophet Ezekiel. Ezekiel was a prophet during the Babylonian captivity when Israel's despair and hopelessness had sunk to new depths. They felt as if they were dead. Ezekiel had a vision in which Yahweh spoke to him. In the vision the people of Israel are symbolized by a valley filled with dry bones. They are dead. Not only has the breath gone out from them, but their corpses have rotted to the bone. However, not even death can limit the power of Yahweh:

> The hand of Yahweh was laid on me, and he carried me away by the spirit (*ruah*) of Yahweh and set me down in the middle of a valley full of bones. He made me walk up and down among them. There were vast quantities of these bones on the ground the whole length of the valley; and they were quite dried up. He said to me, "Son of Man, can these bones live?" I said, "You know, Lord Yahweh." He said, "Prophesy over these bones. Say, 'Dry bones, hear the word of Yahweh. The Lord Yahweh says this to these bones; I am now going to make the breath (*ruah*) enter into you, and you will live. I shall put sinews on you and make you grow flesh. I shall cover you with skin and give you breath, and you will live; and you will learn that I am Yahweh.' " . . . Then he said,

"Son of man, these bones are the whole house of Israel. They keep saying, 'Our bones are dried up, our hope has gone; we are as good as dead.' The Lord Yahweh says this; I am now going to open your graves. . . . I shall put my spirit in you and you shall live" (Ez 37:1–6, 11, 14).

Ezekiel's great vision shows that it is God who is in control of creation. God did not simply create the world and take a vacation for several million years. God remains intimately involved in his creation, and for this reason his creation will eventually fulfill the purposes for which it has been created. Nothing can prevent this—not even death.

We can conclude this from what we have had to say about the different ways in which the Israelites came to understand their God. Did God change? Was he at one time a stern judge who eventually mellowed over the years into a God of compassion? Of course not. Rather what we have been able to see is that the Israelite understanding of Yahweh developed. It will take hundreds of years for the Israelites to more fully discover what they have found in Yahweh—a discovery that is not fully complete until the death and resurrection of Jesus.

For Personal Reflection

1. Unlike Ezekiel, you have probably never seen a valley of dry bones come back to life. But perhaps you have felt lonely or depressed and there was someone there to pick you up. Have you ever gone through a very difficult period of time and felt as if there was no hope in sight? Who are the people you turn to at such times? Do you think that God could be working through these people?

2. In what ways has your own understanding of God changed as you have matured? Sometimes periods of doubt or confusion

may represent a need for a deeper understanding of God. Have you experienced times such as these that led you to a deeper understanding of God?

Questions for Review

1. What does the name "Yahweh" mean? What does it reveal to us about God?

2. In what sense is the discovery of Yahweh like the discovery of America?

3. What was the exodus? In what way was Yahweh understood as a Savior from this experience?

4. How does the Bible reflect the inspiration of God and the abilities of man?

5. What was the covenant between Yahweh and Israel? How did Jeremiah envision this covenant?

6. What does Amos say about religious people who ignore the needs of the poor?

7. What was the Babylonian captivity? Why was it such a devastating experience for the Jews? What message does Isaiah bring to these despairing people?

8. What is the significance of the Hebrew word *ruah?* How are the wind and spirit related?

9. What was Ezekiel's vision and its meaning?

2

Genesis 1–11

T he year is approximately 500 B.C. An Israelite priest lies in his bed and ponders the events that have taken place and the effects that they are having on his people. For many years they had been in exile. Their oppressors had many gods different than the God of Israel. It is time to retell the story of Yahweh and his creation.

He rises from his bed and walks out into the cool morning. It is growing light although the sun has not yet risen. The stars and the moon are still visible. He takes a close, careful look at God's creation. What does he see? The earth is obviously a flat plane. That much is apparent to anyone. Above the earth is a bowl-shaped "firmament" or sky which is dominated by two great "lights," the sun and the moon. Above the sky are the waters that escape from time to time and rain down on the earth. He remembers the stories that he has heard, and he returns to his scroll and begins to write:

> In the beginning, God created the heavens and the earth. Now the earth was a formless void, there was darkness over the deep, and God's spirit hovered over the water.
>
> God said, "Let there be light," and there was light. God saw that light was good and divided light from darkness. God

called the light "day," and the darkness he called "night." Evening came and morning came: the first day.

God said, "Let there be a vault in the waters to divide the waters in two." And so it was. God made the vault and it divided the waters above the vault from the waters below the vault. God called the vault "heaven." Evening came and morning came: the second day.

God said, "Let the waters under heaven come together in a single mass, and let dry land appear. And so it was. God called the dry land "earth" and the mass of waters "seas" and God saw that it was good.

God said, "Let the earth produce vegetation: seed-bearing plants, and fruit trees bearing fruit with their seed inside, on the earth. And so it was. The earth produced vegetation: plants bearing seed in their several kinds, and trees bearing fruit with their seeds inside in their several kinds. God saw that it was good. Evening came and morning came: the third day.

God said, "Let there be lights in the vault of heaven to divide day from night, and let them indicate festivals, days and years. Let there be lights in the vault of heaven to shine on the earth." And so it was. God made the two great lights: the greater light to govern the day, the smaller light to govern the night, and the stars. God set them in the vault of heaven to shine on the earth, to govern the day and the night and to divide light from darkness. God saw that it was good. Evening came and morning came: the fourth day.

God said, "Let the waters teem with living creatures, and let birds fly above the earth within the vault of heaven." And so it was. God created great serpents and every kind of living creature with which the waters teem, and every kind of winged creature. God saw that it was good. God blessed them, saying, "Be fruitful, multiply and fill the waters of the seas; and let the birds multiply upon the earth." Evening came and morning came: the fifth day.

God said: "Let the earth produce every kind of living creature: cattle, reptiles and every kind of wild beast." And so it was. God made every kind of wild beast, every kind of cattle, and every kind of land reptile. God saw that it was good.

God said, "Let us make man in our own image, in the likeness of ourselves, and let them be masters of the fish of the sea, the birds of heaven, the cattle, all the wild beasts and all the reptiles that crawl upon the earth."

> God created man in the image of himself,
> in the image of God he created him,
> male and female he created them.

God blessed them saying, "Be fruitful, multiply, fill the earth and conquer it. Be masters of the fish of the sea, the birds of heaven and all the living animals on the earth." God said, See, I give you all the seed-bearing plants that are upon the whole earth, and all the trees with seed-bearing fruit; this shall be your food. To all wild beasts, all birds of heaven and all living reptiles on the earth I give all the foliage of plants for food." And so it was. God saw all he had made and indeed it was very good. Evening came and morning came: the sixth day.

Thus heaven and earth were completed with all their array. On the seventh day, God completed the work he had been doing. He rested on the seventh day after all the work he had been doing. God blessed the seventh day and made it holy, because on that day he had rested after all his work of creating.

Such were the origins of heaven and earth when they were created (Gen 1:1–2:4a).

More than two thousand years later, this story of creation continues to be widely known and read throughout the world. There are those, however, who scoff at the story. "The story cannot be true," they say, "because the overwhelming scientific evidence points to an evolutionary creation that took place over millions of years.'' To accept the story in Genesis for them is to reject human intelligence and knowledge. In a way, of course, these people are correct. If we read this creation account as a *scientific* teaching, then it is an inaccurate and primitive view of the world. However, the inspired meaning of the story is not the scientific one. The biblical authors described the world as they saw and understood it. The message and truth that they mean to communicate are religious ones. They are not interested in explaining how God creates, but they are intent on explaining the meaning and purpose of the creation. These are two very different levels of questions:

the scientific question: How was the universe created? (We are still only scratching the surface of the answer to this question.)

the religious question: Why does the universe exist? Is there meaning and purpose behind it? What role and meaning do human beings have?

The creation account that we just examined sheds very little light on the first question. Let's examine what it has to say about the religious question.

1. *The universe is the result of God's creative power.* In this creation account the author emphasizes the great power of God. God speaks and his word has power: ''God said, 'Let there be light, and there was light.' '' Religiously, it is unimportant whether God created the world in seven days or if it is in a state of creative evolution. Either way, the creation is the result of God's power at work. (Some people get upset at the thought of evolution. They believe that it takes God out of the process. This is not true. Many scientists believe the evolutionary process to be the result of a miraculously sublime intelligence behind the creation.)

2. *God's creation is good.* Some religions see the earth and the body as a prison from which human beings must escape in order to achieve true freedom. Others believe that the world is basically sinful or evil. This is not the biblical viewpoint. The author stresses this point. Six times in the creation account, God looked at the work that he had done and saw how good it was.

3. *Human beings are given responsibility over the creation.* According to this author, human beings are made in ''the image and likeness of God.'' Humans represent the pinnacle of God's creation. But how are humans made in God's image and likeness? Does this mean that we look like God? The answer is contained in the very next line of Scripture: ''God blessed them, saying, 'Be fruitful, multiply, fill the earth and conquer it. Be masters of the fish of the sea, the birds of heaven and all the living animals on earth.' '' Humans are given the responsibility to continue the work of creation. We share in God's image in that he allows us to become co-creators with him. This refers to bringing more than children into the world. It means bringing goodness, beauty, love and justice into the world as well.

If we read this creation account for what it is—religious teaching—we can see that, in fact, its truth is profound. We can see why men and women still read the story thousands of years later. The story of creation sheds light on the great human and religious question: Why do we and the universe exist?

For Personal Reflection

1. In order to appreciate the religious dimension of the creation from a different perspective, listen to Cat Stevens' ''Morning Has Broken'' (Tea for the Tillerman album).

2. In what ways do you think that humans have been faithful to their responsibility over creation? How is the world a better place? How have we failed in this responsibility?

The Second Story of Creation

At the time when Yahweh God made earth and heaven there was as yet no wild bush on the earth nor had any wild plant sprung up, for Yahweh God had not sent the rain on the earth, nor was there any man to till the soil. However a flood was rising from the earth and watering all the surface of the soil. Yahweh fashioned man of dust from the soil. Then he breathed into his nostrils a breath of life, and thus man became a living being (Gen 2:4b–7).

As you can see, there are actually two creation accounts in the Book of Genesis. The second one immediately follows the first. In fact, it is believed that the second account is based on stories much older than the first. In this second account, we see God form man from the clay of the earth and breathe life into him. In this version of the creation the emphasis is placed on the creation of man and on the need for partnership. Man (the Hebrew word *adam* means man) is created first, and all else is created for his benefit. However, none of the creation fills the man's deepest longings until there is creation of another human being:

Yahweh God said, "It is not good that the man should be alone. I will make him a helpmate." So from the soil Yahweh God fashioned all the wild beasts and all the birds of heaven. These he brought to the man to see what he would call them; each one was to bear the name the man would give it. The man gave names to all the cattle, all the birds of heaven and all the wild beasts. But no helpmate suitable for man was found for him. So Yahweh God made the man fall into a deep

sleep. And while he slept, he took one of the ribs and enclosed
it in flesh. Yahweh God built the rib he had taken from the
man into a woman, and brought her to the man. The man ex-
claimed:

> "This at last is bone from my bones,
> and flesh from my flesh!
> This is to be called woman,
> for this was taken from man."

This is why man leaves his father and mother and joins
himself to his wife, and they become one body.

Now both of them were naked, the man and his wife,
but they felt no shame in front of each other (Gen 2:18–25).

Woman, alone among all the creation, is a suitable partner
for the man. This passage is a beautiful affirmation of our human
sexuality. Man and woman have been created for each other. The
qualities of their masculine and feminine personalities are meant
to enhance and compliment each other. If we look back to the first
creation account we read: "In the divine image he created him,
male and female he created them." We see the divine image reflected in male and female—not one alone. The harmony and in-
timacy that the sexes were created for is reflected in the last line
of the second account: "Now both of them were naked, the man
and his wife, but they felt no shame in front of each other." This
second account reflects the harmony that God desires to exist in
our relationships.

For Personal Reflection

The second creation account affirms our sexuality as something beautiful. Sexuality is more than sexual intercourse. It is our
entire self as either male or female. It includes the way we think,

feel and act. What do you think are the personality differences between men and women? Are we born with these differences or do we learn them?

Sin And Evil

The Israelite editors are smiling. The creation accounts are truly masterpieces—beautifully written, eloquent, rich in meaning and insight. These stories will take their place among the greatest in the history of mankind. However, there is a big problem. The main theme of these stories is that God has created out of goodness and his creation reflects that goodness. But who would believe it? The world is filled with hatred, war, deceit and evil of all kinds. More must be written. Somehow they must explain the presence of sin and evil in the world. And the story continues:

> The serpent was the most subtle of all the wild beasts that Yahweh God had made. It asked the woman: "Did God really say that you were not to eat of any of the trees in the garden?" The woman answered the serpent, "We may eat the fruit of the trees in the garden. But of the fruit of the tree in the middle of the garden God said, 'You must not eat it, nor touch it, under pain of death!' " Then the serpent said to the woman, "No. You will not die! God knows in fact that on the day you eat it your eyes will be opened and you will be like gods, knowing good and evil." The woman saw that the tree was good to eat and pleasing to the eye, and that it was desirable for the knowledge it could give. She took some of its fruit and ate it. She gave some also to her husband who was with her, and he ate it. Then the eyes of both were opened, and they realized that they were naked. So they sewed fig leaves together to make themselves loincloths (Gen 3:1–7).

As we can see from the story, life begins to go badly when people rebel against God. The author of this story describes our sinfulness symbolically. The serpent is the symbol of evil and selfishness. He lures them into putting their trust in him and not God. The temptation he offers is an interesting one. The serpent tells them, "You will be like gods." The author is giving us an insight into the nature of sin. Sin is a rejection of our true selves. We are creatures who are limited. The world does not revolve around me. Often sin occurs because we do not want to accept our creaturely status. We want to be the center of the world. That's what the serpent offers Adam and Eve, and they give in to the temptation.

Immediately we are able to see the effects of sin in the story. The couple realize that they are naked and they sew fig leaves to hide their nakedness. The natural and beautiful harmony that existed between them has been destroyed. The man blames the woman for the sin. Life is beginning to break down. The sin of Adam and Eve is not limited to themselves. There now exists a "state of sin," and the evil is growing worse. The children of Adam and Eve are unable to live in harmony. Cain kills Abel out of jealousy. Sin is spreading.

But this cannot be the end of the story. What has happened to the great God who created the world to reflect his goodness? Does he not care about the earth anymore? Has he abandoned man to his own devices? The story continues:

> Yahweh saw that the wickedness of man was great on the earth and that the thoughts in his heart fashioned nothing but wickedness all day long. Yahweh regretted having made man on the earth, and his heart grieved. "I will rid the earth's face of man, my own creation," Yahweh said, "and of animals also, reptiles too and the birds of heaven: for I regret having made them." But Noah found favor with the Lord (Gen 6:5–8).

You know the rest of the story: the ark, the animals two by two and the flood. But what is the story supposed to mean? If we get God angry he will drown us? Is this a story of God's vengeance? Actually, the story of Noah is a story of hope—that in the face of intolerable evil and sin God does not abandon man. He makes a covenant with Noah and his family, and through them he renews his relationship with mankind. The God who created the world out of love will not abandon the people he has created. God is always offering us a new beginning. God continues to renew the earth.

For Personal Reflection

In the story of Adam and Eve, we saw that sin is a failure to accept ourselves as we really are. The good news of Christ is that we are loved by God the way we are with all our limitations and imperfections. What do you find most difficult to accept about yourself? Do you make that weakness the basis of your self-worth or can you put it in perspective with all your good points?

The first eleven chapters of Genesis contain some of the most famous and widely known stories in the world. *These stories, while not factually true, are filled with great truth.* For in these stories we find the Israelite response to the great questions that mankind has always asked: What is the meaning of man? Why is there evil in the world? How did the universe originate? What is the nature of man's relationship to God?

Questions for Review

1. Why would it be wrong to attack the creation accounts as scientifically inaccurate?

2. What is the difference between scientific and religious truth?

3. What are three important religious truths to be found in the first creation account?

4. What is the biblical author teaching about sexuality in the second creation account?

5. According to the Book of Genesis, how do sin and evil enter the world?

6. Why is the story of the flood a story of hope?

3

The Synoptic Gospels

Earlier we mentioned that some of the books of the Bible are more important than others. For a Christian, the Gospels represent the pinnacle of God's word. In the Gospels we come face to face with Jesus as he was known by the early Church. Here we read the narratives about the climax of all salvation history—God becoming man. We see our own lives in the lives of those who struggle to understand and follow Jesus. If we are seriously interested in the message of the Bible and the message of Jesus, it is to the Gospels that we must return over and over again.

Before we look at Matthew, Mark and Luke, there are some important questions that need to be answered. To begin with, what is a Gospel? Is it the same as a biography? How and when were the Gospels written? Why do some of the Gospels have different stories or different details of the same story?

What Is a Gospel?

The Gospels are unique "literary forms." Nothing exactly like them has either preceded or followed them. The most common mistake is to believe that the Gospels are biographies of Jesus. This is not true. A biography is concerned with an accurate portrayal of the facts of a person's life. Strict attention is paid to detail and to accuracy. This is not true with the Gospels. They are much more interested in conveying the *meaning* behind the events of Jesus' life. Their main purpose is not to present facts but to evoke faith. Their hope is that the readers will not only know about Jesus of Nazareth (the facts) but that they will know him in their hearts and follow him.

The Gospels themselves were originally written in Greek, the prominent language in the Middle East in the first century A.D. *Euaggelion* is the Greek word that we translate as "Gospel." *Euaggelion* was a word used in the Roman Empire to mean "tidings of joy" or a "proclamation of good news." Thus, the word "Gospel" is most commonly translated as "good news."

Before the Gospels came into their written form, Jesus preached the Gospel. His message and teaching were "good news." Jesus was by no means a "gloom and doom" preacher. He called his message a Gospel, a reason for great joy and rejoicing.

For Personal Reflection

When was the last time you heard good news? How did it make you feel? Do you think of your religious beliefs as good news, a source of happiness in your life?

How Were the Gospels Written?

A very common misunderstanding that some people have is to believe that the Gospel writers all sat in the presence of Jesus taking notes that they would soon turn into best sellers. This is not how the Gospels came into their written form. They were written long after the death and resurrection of Jesus. Mark's Gospel, the first written, was not completed until about thirty-five years after Jesus had died (about 65–70 A.D.). And John's Gospel was not written until near the end of the first century. Until Mark's version, the Gospel was spread by word of mouth. The events of Jesus' life and the stories that he told were repeated from one group of Christians to the next. Eventually the Gospels were written as texts for the early Church to keep alive the memory of Jesus and to instruct new believers in the faith.

Scholars believe that there also existed another written document older than the Gospels that has not survived. This document apparently contained many of the sayings of Jesus and was used by some of the Gospel authors when writing their texts. This work is known as the "Q" document (from the German word *Quelle* meaning source). When Matthew and Luke wrote their Gospels (about 85 A.D.), they used Mark and the Q document as sources. John's Gospel is distinct from the other three and seems to have used independent sources.

Gospel Formation:

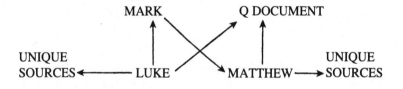

As you can see from this chart, the Gospels of Matthew, Mark and Luke have a great deal in common. For this reason, they are known as the Synoptic Gospels. Synoptic means seen from the same point of view or with the same eye. When you read these Gospels you will notice that there are sections in each that are identical; however each of them also has a good deal of material that is theirs alone and gives their Gospel a unique quality.

For Personal Reflection

The Gospels are ways to keep the memory of Jesus alive. In doing so the church was performing a very human task. Look around your room and recall the different ways in which you keep memories alive. Pictures, posters, letters and diaries are probably among your most valuable possessions. Many of these things are able to help us feel the presence of people who may be very far away. At their best the Gospels bring us the very presence of Christ.

Why Four Gospels?

Many people have wondered why the Church included four Gospels in its collection of sacred writings. Why not just choose the best one? In fact, there were more than four written. The Church had to decide to limit itself to four. The leaders of the Christian community faced a decision. Which of the writings should be included in the Bible? By deciding on these four Gospels, the Church was saying that they accurately and truthfully reflected the faith of the community. Some of the other Gospels were rejected because they were not true reflections of Christian belief. For example, one of the rejected Gospels emphasized the divinity of Jesus but completely neglected the human dimension of his personality.

There is also an advantage to choosing four Gospels rather than one. By having four Gospels, the Church has a multi-faceted look at Jesus. In each Gospel the person is the same (Jesus), but the author's viewpoint is somewhat different. What we come away with is a richer, fuller understanding of Christ.

The Gospel of Mark

Mark's Gospel is written in approximately the year 70. It is written to a Church that has seen its greatest leaders, Peter, Paul and James, all put to death. It is written to a Church suffering persecution from the Roman Empire. When Mark writes his Gospel, he must make it clear to his readers that their faith must exist in the midst of suffering, and that their faith is not a protection from suffering. He must somehow convey to them a message of ''good news'' and show them that not even their Savior was exempt from suffering.

Mark's Gospel is the only one of the four that does not begin with a lengthy message about the divine origin of Jesus. In Matthew and Luke we have the stories of Jesus' birth and in John we have the prologue (a poem-hymn that identifies Jesus with God). Mark's Gospel has no such introduction. It picks up in the middle of Jesus' life. Jesus is already a man being baptized by John the Baptist: ''And a voice came from heaven, 'You are my Son the Beloved, my favor rests on you' '' (Mk 1:11). But the voice is only heard by Jesus. No one else is aware of his identity. Mark's Gospel is written like a mystery story. What we are able to see over the first eight chapters of Mark's Gospel is Jesus performing miracles and preaching but not revealing his special identity and mission. Throughout the Gospel the people are constantly in awe and wonder who this man is.

> They went as far as Capernaum and as soon as the sabbath came he went to the synagogue and began to teach. And his teaching made a deep impression on them because, unlike the scribes, he taught with authority. In their synagogue just then there was a man who was possessed by an unclean spirit, and it shouted, ''What do you want with us, Jesus of Nazareth? Have you come to destroy us? I know who you are: the Holy

One of God.'' But Jesus said sharply, ''Be quiet! Come out
of him!'' And the unclean spirit threw the man into convul-
sions and with a loud cry came out of him. The people were
so astonished that they started asking each other what it all
meant. ''Here is a teaching that is new,'' they said, ''and with
authority behind it: he gives orders even to unclean spirits and
they obey him.''

Even his relatives (we are not sure who Mark is referring to)
don't know what to make of him: ''He went home again and once
more such a crowd collected that he could not even have a meal.
When his relatives heard of this, they set out to take charge of him,
convinced that he was out of his mind'' (Mk 3:20–21). The apostles follow him but even they are unaware of who he is. This is
made clear when they are in a boat with Jesus in the midst of a
storm.

But he was in the stern, his head on a cushion, asleep. They
woke him up and said to him, ''Master, do you not care? We
are going down!'' And he woke up and rebuked the wind and
said to the sea, ''Quiet now! Be calm!'' And the wind
dropped and all was calm again. Then he said to them, ''Why
are you so frightened? How is it that you have no faith?''
They were filled with awe and said to one another, ''*Who can
this be?* Even the wind and the sea obey him.''

Mark's great mystery reaches its climax in the middle of his
Gospel, Chapter 8. Jesus turns to his disciples and says, ''Who
do men say that I am?'' It is finally time to begin to answer the
riddle. The disciples respond with the most current explanations
of Jesus. He is a prophet or perhaps Elijah or John the Baptist
come back from the dead. Jesus then turns the question to them:
''Who do you say that I am?'' Have they understood any better
than the crowds? Peter comes through with the answer: ''You are
the Christ.'' He appears to understand, but Jesus will not leave it

at this. "He began to teach them that the Son of Man was destined to suffer grievously, to be rejected by the chief priests and elders and the scribes, and to be put to death, and after three days to rise again" (Mk 8:31–32). Peter will not hear of this. Like everyone else, he has yet to understand. He expects the Messiah to be triumphant. However, Jesus is the Messiah who finds his glory not in power but in self-sacrifice and in giving. In a world scarred with evil, Jesus is the Messiah who must suffer. Jesus remains reluctant to accept the title Messiah because he knows of all the false expectations that go with it.

The final chapters of Mark's Gospel concern themselves with Jesus' instructions to his apostles and his going to Jerusalem where he will suffer and die. Throughout these chapters the disciples continue to miss the point. They still see Jesus' mission in terms of power and achievement. Perhaps the ultimate irony is the story that Mark tells about James and John and their struggle for power:

> James and John, the sons of Zebedee approached him. "Master," they said to him, "we want you to do us a favor." He said to them, "What is it that you want me to do for you?" They said to him, "Allow us to sit one at your right hand and one at your left hand in glory." . . .
>
> When the other ten heard this they began to feel indignant with James and John, so Jesus called them to him and said to them, "You know that among the pagans their so-called rulers lord it over them, and their great men make their authority felt. This is not to happen among you. No, anyone who wants to become great among you must become the servant, anyone who wants to be the first among you must become the slave to all. For the Son of Man did not come to be served but to serve, and to give his life as a ransom for many (Mk 10:35–37, 41–45).

What is the portrait of Jesus that Mark has presented to us? It is the picture of a man who will not accept the worldly understanding of success and power. For Mark, the Messiah must keep his identity a secret because he is not the Messiah that everyone anticipates. For those who read Mark's Gospel in the midst of Roman persecution, it is clear that in order to follow Jesus they must go through the same path of self-surrender.

Today it is very difficult to take Mark's picture of Jesus too seriously. The culture that we live in offers us a different lifestyle to follow—one filled with power and success. Most of us are more like Peter. We want power over the situation. We find it very difficult to love to the point of suffering. Yet this is what the Gospel asks us to strive for.

For Personal Reflection

1. Suffering is one of the biggest problems of religious faith. Why does God permit it? Whatever the answer, Jesus is not immune from it. Has suffering ever been an obstacle to your faith? Has there ever been a time when you felt that your faith helped you in a time of suffering? Does suffering ever have any good consequences?

2. Can you think of examples within your own family when love has included suffering?

The Gospel of Matthew

When Matthew writes his Gospel, he has Mark's as a source. He uses Mark's to provide a basic outline of events, but he adds a great deal more of Jesus' teaching. Matthew also precedes these events with the story of the birth of Jesus. Part of the reason for Matthew's additions is that he is writing for a different audience. The Church for whom Matthew writes is composed mostly of Christians who have converted from Judaism. Thus, Matthew is very concerned with showing that Jesus is the fulfillment of Judaism. According to Matthew, Jesus is the new Moses who brings a new law, the law of love. The followers of Jesus are to be the new Israel, the new community of salvation.

Matthew begins his Gospel with a genealogy tracing the ancestry of Jesus. This genealogy is not meant to be an accurate listing of Jesus' family tree. The purpose of the genealogy is symbolic. It is meant to connect Jesus with the salvation history of Israel. Thus Matthew carefully connects Jesus' heritage to David and then to Abraham the father of Jewish faith. Matthew is making a very definite point: what had begun with Abraham is fulfilled in Jesus.

Both Matthew and Luke include what we call the infancy narratives. Yet each one tells the story in such a way as to suit his own purposes. Matthew includes the story of King Herod killing all the innocent children in order to prevent Jesus from coming into power. Joseph, Mary and Jesus escape into Egypt and return only after Herod's death. This story closely parallels the story of Moses who must escape from a tyrant and who returns from exile to save his people (Ex 1—3). This is no coincidence. Matthew is beginning to draw a comparison between Moses and Jesus. Also in his brief infancy narrative, Matthew goes to great lengths to show how the birth of Jesus is the fulfillment of the Old Testament. For example, his description of the virgin birth: ''Now all this took place to fulfill the words spoken by the Lord to the prophet: 'The virgin shall conceive and give birth to a son and they shall call him Immanuel' '' (Mt 1:22—23). The quote that Matthew chooses is from the prophet Isaiah. Matthew means to show Jesus as the fulfillment of the verse. He uses this technique four other times in the infancy narrative alone and continuously throughout his Gospel.

Probably the most famous parts of Matthew's Gospel are his classic Chapters 5—7 which are known as the Sermon on the Mount. In these chapters, Matthew brilliantly summarizes the teachings of Jesus. Here we find the Beatitudes, the Lord's Prayer and the Golden Rule, passages that are universally known and revered. Again Matthew compares Jesus to Moses. Like Moses, Jesus goes up the mountain to give his teaching. (Luke has Jesus giving the teaching on a plain because he is unconcerned with the Old Testament symbolism.) Matthew sees the teaching of Jesus as the fulfillment of the Mosaic law. Instead of ten "thou shalt not" Commandments, we find instead the Beatitudes. These Beatitudes are different than the Commandments. They emphasize inner attitudes and positive actions whereas the Commandments tend to emphasize negative prohibitions. Jesus is not interested in giving a list of commands as much as he is in describing the "happy" or "blessed" man. Yet Jesus' description of what it means to be happy is in stark contrast to the happiness that the world often strives for:

> How happy are the poor in spirit;
> theirs is the kingdom of heaven.
> Happy the gentle;
> they shall have the earth for their heritage.
> Happy those who mourn;
> they shall be comforted.
> Happy those who hunger and thirst for what is right;
> they shall be satisfied.
> Happy the merciful;
> they shall have mercy shown them.
> Happy the pure in heart;
> they shall see God.
> Happy the peacemakers;
> they shall be called sons of God.
> Happy those who are persecuted in the cause of right;
> theirs is the kingdom of heaven.

Some of the phrases and expressions used are unclear to twentieth century minds. Let's take a closer look at the meaning of these Beatitudes.

Happy are the poor in spirit. Who are the "poor in spirit"? It is not a figure of speech that we would use to describe someone. Perhaps the best word that we have today to translate this word is humility. Humility is sometimes understood as putting oneself down, but that is not its true meaning. The humble see themselves as they truly are. They recognize their strengths and their weaknesses and they realize that everything that they have is a gift. The "poor in spirit" are the opposite of the proud—those who are so taken with their own self-importance that they are oblivious to the needs of others. The poor in spirit recognize that they are not the center of the universe and that the greatest person is always totally dependent on God.

Happy are the gentle (or the meek as it is sometimes translated). The gentle are much like the poor in spirit. They are open and accepting of others. The gentle know the warmth of God's love and communicate it to others. The opposite of the gentle are the violent or the abusive—those whose self-hatred cannot be confined to themselves.

Happy are those who mourn. This Beatitude certainly seems to be the strangest of all. It seems to be saying, "Happy are the unhappy." In fact, this is not its meaning, but it does make us face a very important element of the Beatitudes. The happiness that Jesus has to offer is not fulfillment or success as the world generally understands it. It is the happiness that comes with openness and obedience to the will of God. Why are those who mourn happy? Because they are those who have been willing to enter into the suffering involved in life. Those who mourn are those who feel deeply and care deeply enough to hurt. The superficial pleasure-seeker never really has his heart broken because he has been unable to give it away. It is only those who mourn who learn the compassion at the heart of God's love.

Happy are those who hunger and thirst for what is right. What do we hunger and thirst for? All the latest fashions and games? Security? Pleasure? Money? Those who find their happiness in God are the ones who hunger and thirst for what is right. Their overriding concern is always justice and integrity. This Beatitude has a power to it. The follower of Jesus is not a milk-toast do-gooder, but a person who passionately seeks justice.

Happy are the merciful. If there is a Beatitude that should not surprise us, it is probably this one. Jesus is very clearly the champion of God's mercy. It is to be extended to the poor, the sick, the outcast and the sinner. It is also a striking contrast to the attitude of many of the Pharisees of Jesus' time who saw themselves as righteous and were scornful of sinners.

Happy are the pure in heart. The explanation sometimes given of this Beatitude is that Jesus is referring to sexual purity. There is really no indication of that. Instead, this Beatitude seems to refer to a certain single-mindedness in our love for God. It implies a devotion and heartfelt commitment to God. The opposite of purity of heart is a flip-flopping allegiance to God whenever it suits our own needs or purposes. The pure in heart are those whose love for God is the number one drive and commitment in their life.

Happy are the peacemakers. Recently in the Catholic Church, there has been a renewed emphasis on the spirit of this Beatitude. The bishops of the Church clearly recognize that the task of Christians should be an active one in this world. They are to be peacemakers. The U.S. Catholic bishops considered this to be such an important issue that they spent three years researching the issue for a pastoral letter published in 1983 entitled "The Challenge of Peace." It is an excellent example of how the Beatitudes of Jesus must be made real in each age and society.

Happy are those persecuted in the cause of right. This final Beatitude again reverses the wisdom that the world offers us to be careful and to watch out for ourselves first. Persecution is certainly not something to be sought after, but it is the blessed man who will ultimately endure it for the sake of what is right.

For Personal Reflection

1. Which of the Beatitudes do you think is most in need of being heeded by the world in which we live?

2. What practical changes would you have to make in your life to truly become a "Beatitude person"?

In a sense, Matthew's list of Beatitudes are the new Commandments for the new Israel, the Church. They describe the type of life the Christian is called to live. On further examination, they also give us a great deal of insight into the person of Jesus. For it is Christ who embodies each of the Beatitudes. By using the Beatitudes and Jesus as a model, Matthew tells us that the Christian will become the salt of the earth and the light of the world.

> You are the salt of the earth. But if salt becomes tasteless, what can make it salty again? It is good for nothing and can only be thrown out to be trampled underfoot by men.
> You are the light of the world. A city built on a hilltop cannot be hidden. No one lights a lamp to put it under a tub; they put it on a lampstand were it shines for everyone in the house. In the same way your light must shine among men, so that seeing your good works, they may give praise to your Father in heaven (Mt 5:13–16).

Matthew uses two powerful symbols from his world to explain the role of the Church. The first is that of salt. In those days there was no refrigeration and salt was used to keep meat fresh. Thus, the role of the Church is to keep the world "fresh" and stop it from "going bad." The second image for the Church is that of light. Today all we have to do is flip a switch and we have light, but of course this was not the situation two thousand years ago. At night the lamp was placed in the middle of the house. Outside, in the darkness, there were no street lights and only a brave man or a fool would travel the roads when the sun went down. But in the light one can see clearly. In a world of darkness and confusion, the Church is to be a light, a beacon of truth. Its goodness, charity and justice is to attract men and women out of the darkness of sin.

In summary, Matthew's Gospel is concerned with showing a Jewish/Christian audience that Jesus is the fulfillment of the history of Israel. He is the new Moses, the great new teacher who fulfills the Mosaic law. Matthew, however, is equally concerned with describing the Church, the new Israel. The new community of salvation must be a Beatitude people and a light to the world.

For Personal Reflection

Can you think of any ways in which the Church today is truly a light to the world?

The Gospel of Luke

Jesus Christ—when we say the Lord's name, we seem to imply that his first name is Jesus and his last name is Christ, like Bob Smith or Mary Jones. However, the word Christ is not a name as much as it is a title. Jesus Christ is really Jesus the Christ. The word "Christ" is simply the Greek translation of the Hebrew Messiah. Jesus Christ is in fact a statement of faith. It was only after the resurrection that it finally became clear to the followers of Jesus that he was the Messiah and the Lord and Savior.

Before long, however, the Church had a problem to solve. Was Jesus the Messiah and Savior of Israel or is he the Savior of all mankind? At first, this was not an issue. The whole notion of Messiah was one that made sense only to the Jews and their unique religious history. The earliest Christians still saw themselves as a part of Judaism and continued to worship in the synagogue and temple. The problem arose when Gentiles (non-Jews) began to accept Jesus. Gradually the Church began to see that Jesus was the Savior of all people. The good news of salvation extended beyond the Jews to the whole world.

This great new fact was one of the main ideas behind the writing of St. Luke. In the New Testament, there are two works by Luke: his Gospel and the Acts of the Apostles. In these two volumes, Luke traces salvation history from Bethlehem (Jesus' birthplace) to Jerusalem (the scene of the resurrection and the early Church) and ultimately to Rome, the center of the Gentile world. In his Gospel Luke emphasizes the fact that salvation comes in the most unexpected places. The Jews, proud of their great religious heritage, are in danger of missing the moment of salvation. It is most especially the scribes and Pharisees, the teachers and the devout, who are most in jeopardy. They looked down on the outcasts, the sinners, the Gentiles, and those who do not follow the law strictly. Luke's message is that it was these outcasts who were receiving God's offer of salvation.

Luke's concerns can be seen from the onset of the Gospel. His infancy narrative has an entirely different tone than Matthew's Gospel. Mary is the hero of Luke's story. She is the humble handmaiden of God. And from the mouth of Mary we hear of God's disdain for the proud and his blessing on the "lowly" :

> My soul proclaims the greatness of the Lord
> and my spirit exults in God my savior;
> because he has looked down upon his lowly handmaid. . . .
> He has shown the power of his arm.
> He has routed the proud of heart (Lk 1:46–47a, 51).

Jesus himself is born in poverty in a manger. His birth is not accompanied by kings (Matthew's version) but by shepherds who were held in disdain by the religious leaders because of their inability to keep all the Jewish ritual laws. Yet it is to them that the angel delivers the message of joy.

When we examine the genealogy in Luke's Gospel (Lk 3:23–38), we can see another important distinction that he makes. Luke traces the "family tree" of Jesus back to Adam. Again, the meaning is symbolic. Just as Matthew traced Jesus' ancestry to Abraham to show that he was the fulfillment of Judaism, Luke traces it to Adam to show that Jesus is the Savior of all mankind. Adam represents humanity itself.

This theme is developed in Jesus' public ministry. Luke makes clear that it is a ministry to the poor and the outcast.

> He came to Nazareth where he had been brought up, and he went into the synagogue on the sabbath day as he usually did. He stood up to read, and they handed him the scroll of the prophet Isaiah. Unrolling the scroll, he found the place where it is written:

> The Spirit of the Lord has been given to me,
> for he has anointed me.
> He has sent me to bring the good news to the poor,
> to proclaim liberty to captives,
> and to the blind new sight,
> to set the downtrodden free,
> to proclaim the Lord's year of favor (Lk 4:16–19).

In this passage, Jesus identifies himself with the anointed one of the Lord who comes to bring salvation to the poor, to captives, to the blind and the downtrodden. Jesus sees his mission as being one of reconciliation. Unfortunately some of the people don't want God's mercy, they want his reward. They want to be told that they are better than everyone else and that they will finally be rewarded for their virtue. Jesus will have none of this. He comes to offer God's love and mercy to all those who will desire it. Luke has some of the most colorful stories in his Gospel that bring home this point. For example, there is the story of the call of Peter which Luke tells much differently than Matthew or Mark. In Luke's version, Peter has been out fishing all day, and caught nothing. He heads back to the shore weary and discouraged. All of a sudden, he is being approached by a man who would like to use his boat. Would he be so kind as to cast out a bit so the man can address the crowds that have hemmed him in at the shoreline. Peter has heard of the man. Some say he is a prophet. Why not? This boat may as well serve someone well this day. When the prophet has finished speaking, he turns to Peter and says, "Throw out your nets." Reluctantly, impatiently, Peter does it, knowing that there are no more fish out there than there were a minute ago. But what's this? More fish than he has caught in a week. He needs help pulling them in. But Jesus is not finished with him yet. Peter knows that he is in the presence of a holy man: "Leave me, Lord, for I am a sinful man." Jesus replies: "Do not be afraid; from now on it is men that you will catch" (see Lk 5:1–10).

All of Luke's readers would know who Peter was—the great leader of the early Church. Luke's point is to show that his origins are very humble: a fisherman who identifies himself as a sinner. Why does Jesus choose Peter? Probably because he recognizes that he is a sinful man. Peter thinks that his sinfulness is an obstacle to follow Jesus. Jesus sees it not as an obstacle but as a prerequisite. It is only the man who knows that he is dependent on God's mercy who will be able to become a disciple.

There is another Simon mentioned in Luke's Gospel. He is a Pharisee. Simon had heard of the young prophet Jesus and invited him to his house for a meal. It was customary at that time to greet one's guest with a kiss and to have the servant wash his dusty feet. Yet no such signs of hospitality were offered to Jesus.

As the meal begins, an uninvited guest arrives. She is a woman with a "bad name" in town. She falls at the feet of Jesus and weeps. Her heart is broken. She can bear the weight of her sins no longer. Her tears fall on the feet of Jesus. Her hair wipes them dry. She anoints his feet with ointment.

Simon the Pharisee is indignant. Jesus must be a fraud. If he were a real prophet he would never allow such a woman as this to touch him. Jesus says to Simon. "She has shown me all the signs of love that you neglected. She loves because she knows what it means to be loved—to be forgiven her sins." Simon believes himself to be perfect. He need not be loved or forgiven—that would be a sign of weakness. Jesus has nothing to offer him. Jesus turns to the woman and says, "Your faith has saved you, go in peace" (see Lk 7:36–50). This is a typical Lukan story. The apparent good guy (Simon) misses the meaning of Jesus completely, and the apparent villain (the sinful woman) repents and finds salvation.

The same theme can be found in the parable of the good Samaritan. This parable is so well known that the expression "a good Samaritan" is used to apply today to anyone who does a good deed. However, to get the real impact of the story, we have to go back to the time and place in which it was told. A lawyer asks Jesus, "What must I do to inherit eternal life?" He is an expert in Jewish law. If anyone should know the answer to the question it would be he. Yet the story says that he was eager to justify himself. Like Simon the Pharisee, he seems more interested in impressing Jesus than in learning. When Jesus replies that he must love God and neighbor, he responds, "And who is my neighbor?" At the time of Jesus most Jews understood this to mean that they must love their fellow Jews. Rather than give the man an answer, Jesus tells a story. It takes place on the road from Jerusalem to Jericho, a road that his listeners are familiar with and one that is famous for its treachery. A man is robbed, beaten and left in a ditch. Two Jews come by, both members of Israel's religious class, a priest and a Levite. They pass by the man. Now comes the catch to the story. To the rescue comes a Samaritan. Jesus could not have picked a more despised character. The Samaritans were considered religious outcasts who had intermarried with pagans and desecrated the Jewish temple. The Samaritan brings the man to an inn and pays to have him taken care of. Jesus turns the question on the lawyer, "Which of the three was neighbor to the beaten man?" The lawyer won't even say the word. He responds, "The one who took pity on him." Jesus says to him, "Go and do the same yourself."

Luke uses these great stories—the infancy narratives, the call of Peter, Simon and the sinful woman and the good Samaritan—to help spell out his great message: there are no limits or boundaries to the saving love of God!

For Personal Reflection

1. "Peter thinks that his sinfulness is an obstacle to following Jesus. Jesus sees it not as an obstacle but as a prerequisite." What do you think is meant by this? How can we use our limitations as a copout?

2. Luke's Gospel emphasizes that God's love knows no boundaries. How can our society reflect that vision?

3. The Synoptics present three images of Jesus: the suffering servant, the great and wise teacher and the friend of the outcast and sinner. Which of the three do you relate to best?

Questions for Review

1. What is the difference between a Gospel and a biography?

2. In what language were the Gospels originally written?

3. What does the word "Gospel" mean?

4. When was each of the Gospels written?

5. What is the Q document?

6. Which are the Synoptic Gospels? Why are they called that?

7. What does Mark emphasize about Jesus? To whom is he writing and how does that affect his theme?

8. Why is Mark's Gospel like a mystery?

9. When Peter declares Jesus to be the Messiah, what type of Messiah is he thinking of? How is Jesus' understanding different?

10. For whom does Matthew write his Gospel? How does it affect his main themes?

11. Why are the genealogies of Matthew and Luke different? What is each trying to say about Jesus?

12. To whom does Matthew compare Jesus in the story of his birth?

13. What does the term ''poor in spirit'' mean?

14. What does the word ''Christ'' mean?

15. How do the infancy narratives reflect Luke's main theme?

16. In the parable of the good Samaritan, why is it surprising that Jesus chooses a Samaritan to be the ''good guy''?

4

Jesus: Yahweh in Person

In the first chapter of this book we discussed the changing understanding of Yahweh that took place in Israel's history. We focused on the different images of God and on the significance of his name. In this chapter, we would like to re-examine those images in light of how they are understood by Jesus.

The Name of God

The name that Jesus uses to refer to God is, like Yahweh, filled with meaning. The word that Jesus used is an Aramaic one, "Abba." It is a term of loving affection for one's father. It is often translated "father," but it is probably more accurate to say "dad" or "pop." This word that Jesus uses is very different than Yahweh. Yahweh speaks of God's infinite greatness and power over all things. Jews were not even allowed to say the word because of its sacred character. "Abba," on the other hand, speaks of God's love, care and closeness to his children. A father is someone who loves his children unconditionally. He takes delight in their growth, and his main concern is always their happiness. He provides them with security and a sense of trust. He teaches them what to value in life and what to avoid. He shares with them the wealth of his experience and knowledge. He helps them gain their own independence and freedom. When the time comes, he challenges them to walk on their own, to make their own choices and find their own path, but he never for a moment ceases to be a father whose heart travels with his children in whatever journeys they take. In trying to find a way to decribe the closeness and love of his God, Jesus tells us that he is an ''Abba.''

For Personal Reflection

1. Jesus describes the Father in greater depth in the story of the prodigal son. Read Luke 15:11–31.

2. How does your relationship with your father reflect your relationship with God? According to your faith and experience, is God more like a father or a mother?

Jesus the Savior

One of the most important characteristics of Yahweh was his saving power. The great event of the exodus was the center of Jewish faith and demonstrated a God who freed men and women from bondage. Every year the Jewish people would re-enact this great event in the celebration of the Passover. The Jews continued to await God's salvation. At the time of Jesus there seemed to be some hope that God would finally send his Messiah to save his people. But who was this Messiah and what type of salvation would he bring?

The word Messiah means ''anointed one,'' and it originally referred to the Jewish king. Anointing was a symbol of being set aside for a special task or mission. The ''anointed ones'' of Israel were to be more than Israel's kings. They were also to be God's special representatives. God had made a covenant with David that through his line of succession he would maintain his relation with the Jewish people. However, before long the Jewish kings became corrupt and shirked their responsibilities as leaders of Israel. The Jewish people lamented: ''How long before God will send a real Messiah?'' Meanwhile Israel was defeated by the Babylonians, the Assyrians, the Greeks and the Romans. They were continually under the domination of another country. How long must they wait? When would salvation finally come to God's chosen people? When would Yahweh send the Messiah?

By the time Jesus was a young man, the Romans had occupied Palestine for many years. In the desert there lived a prophet named John. His message was, ''Repent; the kingdom of God is close at hand.'' What can this mean? Is the day of salvation finally coming? How is God going to act? John spoke these words: ''There stands among you the one who is coming after me, and I am not fit to undo his sandal straps'' (Jn 1:27). Finally Yahweh will save his people. There is great anticipation among the people. Many go to John for baptism to prepare for the great event which is coming.

Soon Jesus begins his mission. But is he the Messiah? He seems to avoid the title and takes on the role of a teacher and prophet. Even the Baptist appears to be confused. What has happened to the mighty power of the Messiah? Could he have been wrong about Jesus? From prison John sends two of his disciples to question Jesus: ''Are you the one who is to come or are we to look for another'' (Lk 7:19)? Jesus responds to these disciples: ''Go back and tell John what you have seen and heard: the blind see again, the lame walk, lepers are cleansed and the deaf hear, the dead are raised to life and the good news is proclaimed to the poor'' (Lk 7:22). It seems that John is expecting some type of dramatic act of God bringing judgment but Jesus preaches mercy and reconciliation. In his actions Jesus is bringing the kingdom of God to earth, but he is not what John or the people are expecting.

Is Jesus the Savior? He is, but unlike Yahweh who saved the people from Egyptian slavery, Jesus has come to save all mankind from the slavery of sin. Jesus challenges the people to change their hearts, for it is within their hearts that they will discover God's gift of salvation. He challenges them to a new way of relating to God and to one another. He exhorts them to become bearers of God's love and mercy. He extends himself to the sick, the poor and sinners so that they may also know the gracious love of God.

Some of the people of Jesus' time missed out on his message because they labored under the wrong understanding of salvation. Two thousand years later, we continue to do the same. Some people look for salvation in military power, others through personal wealth and success. Even religious people often think of salvation as something that occurs when we die. There is certainly some truth in this, but it misses the core of Jesus' call to salvation. God's offer is here and now. It demands a decision on our part. It is not belonging to a certain religious group that guarantees passage through the pearly gates. Salvation is not something that belongs to the elite. It is God's gift that is open to all.

For Personal Reflection

Do you think of salvation as something that occurs before or after death? Do you consider yourself saved or in need of salvation?

Jesus and the Law of Love

As we have already seen, the law represented for the Jews not only guidelines for life but the very path to salvation. In the

Old Testament, there is no sure way to righteousness other than obedience to the law. There are many people today who believe that the Ten Commandments are the center of Christian faith and that the main mission of Jesus was to get everyone to start obeying them. This is simply inaccurate. The Ten Commandments and the law in general are important elements of faith, but they are not the same as faith. Jesus had a different attitude toward the law than most of the religious teachers of his day. Jesus understood that the law is an instrument that should promote love and justice. When asked which of the Commandments is the greatest, Jesus replies, "You must love the Lord your God with all your heart, with all your soul and with all your mind. This is the greatest and the first commandment. The second resembles it: You must love your neighbor as yourself. On these commandments hang the whole law and the prophets as well" (Mt 22:37–40).

Jesus is very clear: the law of love is the supreme law. For Jesus, love is to be the motivation of our actions. He does not dismiss the law as being unimportant. He doesn't mean to say that we shouldn't have laws or that we need not obey existing laws. He knows that the law is important in achieving the will of God. However, Jesus reacts strongly against an attitude that places rigid obedience of the law over the needs of people. The law should benefit man, not imprison him. Thus, Jesus would break some of the religious laws of his time because they were not at the service of people.

> He went again into a synagogue and there was a man there who had a withered hand. And they were watching him to see if he would cure him on the sabbath day, hoping for something to use against him. He said to the man with the withered hand, "Stand up in the middle." Then he said to them, "Is it against the law on the sabbath day to do good or to do evil; to save life or to kill?" But they said nothing. Then, grieved to find them so obstinate, he looked angrily around at them

and said to the man, "Stretch out your hand." He stretched
it out and his hand was better (Mk 3:1–6).

Jesus was angry that the people did not understand the heart
of the law. The law was meant to be an instrument of love and to
serve people. As Jesus put it: "The sabbath was made for man,
not man for the sabbath" (Mk 2:27).

Probably the best and clearest summary of Jesus' attitude to-
ward the law can be found in the Sermon on the Mount (Mt 5–7).
Here Jesus deals with the old law and the new law, the law of
Moses and the law of Christ. Both are important, but the law of
Moses alone is not enough. Jesus lists the old law and then adds
a new challenge to it:

> You have learned how it was said to our ancestors: "You
> must not kill, and if anyone does kill, he must answer for it
> before the court." But I say to you that anyone who is angry
> with his brother will answer for it before the court.
>
> You have learned how it was said, "You must not com-
> mit adultery." But I say to you that if a man looks at a woman
> with lust in his heart, he has already committed adultery in
> his heart.
>
> You have learned how it was said: Eye for eye and tooth
> for tooth. But I say this to you: offer the wicked man no re-
> sistance. On the contrary, if anyone hits you on the right
> cheek offer him the other as well (Mt 5:21–22, 27–28, 38–
> 39).

As we can see from this passage, Jesus was most interested
in what was in people's hearts. Perhaps the most beautiful expression of Jesus's law of love can be found in the Gospel of John. In
this passage, John emphasizes that Jesus offers us a new relationship with God based not on obedience but on love. It is not the
relationship of slave to master, but a relationship of friendship.
The effect of the relationship is not fear but joy. The Lord's re-

lationship to us is not meant to be one that shackles us with rules but frees us with love.

> As the Father has loved me,
> so I have loved you.
> Remain in my love. . . .
> I have told you this so my joy may be in you
> and your joy may be complete.
> This is my commandment:
> love one another
> as I have loved you.
> A man can have no greater love
> than to lay down his life for his friends.
> You are my friends
> if you do what I command you.
> I shall not call you servants anymore
> because a servant does not know his master's business.
> I call you friends
> because I have made known to you
> everything that I have learned from my Father. . .
> What I command you is to love one another (Jn 15:9, 11–15, 17).

For Personal Reflection

St. Augustine once said, "Love and do as you will." What do you think he meant by this? Are there any dangers to this type of thinking? Do you agree with the statement?

Jesus, the Man of Compassion

While he was at dinner in the house it happened that a number of tax collectors and sinners came to sit at the table with Jesus

and his disciples. When the Pharisees saw this, they said to
the disciples, "Why does your master eat with tax collectors
and sinners?" When he heard this he replied, "It is not the
healthy who need a doctor but the sick. Go and learn the
meaning of the words: 'What I want is mercy, not sacrifice.'
And indeed I did not come to call the virtuous but sinners"
(Mt 9:10–13).

As we have already seen and as this passage shows again,
Jesus seems to feel most at home with "sinners." Why does he
not make friends with the religious leaders of the day, the scribes
and the Pharisees? Why is it that the Gospels continually portray
Jesus in the company of the outcasts of society? In fact, in his own
lifetime he seems to have had the nickname, "the friend of sinners."

In the passage above, Jesus identifies himself as a doctor, a
healer. It is the sick who need the doctor and it is to the sick that
Jesus brings the good news of salvation. Many of Jesus' miracles
and much of his teaching have to do with healing, mercy and reconciliation. For Jesus it must be this way. The human race that he
and the Father love so deeply is a wounded human race. It is filled
with the sick and the needy. There are those who suffer physical
maladies: lepers, the blind, the lame and the dying. And there is
a much larger group suffering spiritual and emotional sickness; the
poor, the widow, the lonely, the sinner, the abused, the orphan,
the prostitute. When surrounded by the wounded, Jesus' love
must take the shape of a healing love.

Jesus is well aware of the fact that the whole human race is
a wounded group. All humans without exception are in need of
healing of one sort or another. To be human means to carry around
inside of us all the bumps and bruises that we accumulate over the
course of a lifetime. To be human also means that at every moment we are less than perfect. It means that we have attitudes in
need of change and relationships in need of healing. It was "the

virtuous'' who refused to see this. The people whom Jesus had the most difficulty reaching were those who refused to join the human race and admit their own need for healing. These people had never faced their own wounds and so they were cold to the woundedness of others. As long as they felt this way they could view themselves as superior to the sinner. In his Gospel, John tells a story of how Jesus forced a group of these men to face their own sinfulness:

> At daybreak he appeared in the temple again; and as all the people came to him, he sat down and began to teach them. The scribes and the Pharisees brought a woman along who had been caught in the act of adultery; and making her stand in full view of everybody, they said to Jesus, "Master, this woman was caught in the very act of committing adultery, and Moses has ordered us in the law to condemn women like this to death by stoning. What have you to say?" They asked him this as a test looking for something to use against him. But Jesus bent down and started writing on the ground with his finger. As they persisted with their question he looked up and said, "If there is one of you who has not sinned, let him be the first to throw a stone at her." Then he bent down and wrote on the ground again. When they heard this, they went away one by one, beginning with the eldest, until Jesus was alone with the woman, who remained standing there. He looked up and said, "Woman, where are they? Has no one condemned you?" "No one, sir," she replied. "Neither do I condemn you," said Jesus; "go away and commit this sin no more" (Jn 8:1–11).

The scribes and the Pharisees are trying to trap Jesus. They want to see if he will tell them to disobey the law of Moses. Jesus knows their plans and turns it around on them: "If there is one of you who has not sinned, let him be the first to throw a stone at her." Jesus forces them to look at the situation from a totally dif-

ferent perspective. As long as they are convinced that there is only
one sinner present (the woman) they can persist in stoning her.
But Jesus makes them face their own sinfulness. She is now one
of them. With this recognition comes the beginning of compassion
and mercy. These men have been faced with their own sinfulness,
and because of this they can feel for the sinner who stands in front
of them.

The compassion of Jesus is not only in his mercy and forgiveness but in his identification with the poor and the oppressed.
Jesus confronts us with a new way of regarding the poor, the sick
and the hungry. If we are well off, healthy and well fed, we could
take the attitude that somehow we are better than the poor. Why
don't they get a job? How come they are so lazy? Or we might
feel sorry for them, but we would still be missing the point. To
Jesus, it is in the least expected people and places that we find the
presence of God. The downtrodden reflect in a special way the
presence of a Lord who was himself poor, a criminal who was
eventually put to death by those in authority.

> "When the Son of Man comes in glory, escorted by all the
> angels, then he will take his seat on the throne of glory. All
> the nations will be assembled before him and he will separate
> men from one another the way a shepherd separates the sheep
> from the goats. He will place the sheep on his right hand and
> the goats on his left. Then the king will say to those on his
> right hand, "Come, you whom my Father has blessed, take
> for your heritage the kingdom prepared for you since the
> foundation of the world. For I was hungry and you gave me
> food; I was thirsty and you gave me drink; I was a stranger
> and you made me welcome; naked and you clothed me; sick,
> and you visited me; in prison and you came to see me. Then
> the virtuous will say to him in reply, 'Lord, when did we see
> you hungry and feed you or thirsty and give you drink? When
> did we see you a stranger and make you welcome, naked and
> clothe you, sick or in prison and come to see you?' And the

king will answer, 'I tell you solemnly, insofar as you did it
for the least of my brothers, you did it to me.' "

The compassion of Jesus is the compassion of one who is
truly one of us. There is always a tendency to downplay the humanity of Jesus in the face of his divinity. This passage makes
clear the intimate connection of the human and the divine. Christ
lives in the poorest of God's children. He offers us a new vision
of what it means to be a human being. We are to feed the hungry
and clothe the naked not simply because we feel sorry for them,
but because their dignity as human beings demands it. For Jesus,
compassion is a vision of life that allows us to see the presence of
God in all our brothers and sisters.

For Personal Reflection

1. "When surrounded by the wounded, Jesus' love had to take
   the shape of a healing love." In what ways are you in need of
   healing? When has someone's love helped to heal you?

2. "Insofar as you did it for the least of my brothers, you did it
   for me." What does this line tell us about the mission of the
   Church?

Jesus, the Life-Giving Spirit

One of the most striking features of Jesus' personality is his
ability to change the lives of people. It is possible to read the Gospels as a chronicle of the lives that Jesus turned upside down. It
seems that he is capable of this because he is so fully committed
to the greatest possibilities of being a human being. He is first and
foremost a person who loves deeply. People who encounter him

seem to be touched by a spirit that he embodies. Tax collectors leave their positions of wealth for him. Prostitutes quit their former lives to follow him. Fishermen give up the security of their job to become fishers of men. What is it that lured them to follow Christ? The Lord touches their hearts and changes their lives forever. They have chosen a new possibility in life—the possibility of a life lived for God.

Jesus himself was faced with the same choice. As a man Jesus had to make the choice every human being must make at one time or another: to build the kingdom of God or to build one's own kingdom. In order to open himself to the Spirit of God, Jesus must turn away from other spirits. Matthew tells the story this way:

> Then Jesus was led into the wilderness to be tempted by the devil. He fasted for forty days and forty nights, after which he was very hungry, and the tempter came and said to him, "If you are the Son of God, tell these stones to turn into loaves." But he replied, "Scripture says, 'Man does not live on bread alone but on every word that comes from the mouth of God.' "
>
> The devil then took him to the holy city and made him stand on the parapet of the temple. "If you are the Son of God," he said, "throw yourself down; for Scripture says: 'He will put you in his angels' charge, and they will support you on their hands in case you hurt your foot against a stone.' " Jesus said to him, "Scripture also says, 'You must not put the Lord your God to the test.' "
>
> Next, taking him to a very high mountain, the devil showed him all the kingdoms of the world and their splendor. "I will give you all of these," he said, "if you fall at my feet and worship me." Then Jesus replied, "Be off, Satan! For Scripture says: 'You must worship the Lord your God, and serve him alone.' "
>
> Then the devil left him, and angels appeared and looked after him (Mt 4:1–11).

This account in Matthew's Gospel is a highly symbolic one. Matthew uses the story to portray the inner struggle of Jesus to be faithful to his own conscience and his mission. In all three temptations, Jesus is provoked to use his gifts for his own glory and not the glory of the Father. The spirit that Jesus meets in the desert is the spirit of sin and death. This spirit tempts us with our own egos. It wants us to believe that there is really no point or meaning to life other than satisfying our basic needs. Nothing lasts. Nothing matters. All of our efforts wind up in death.

Jesus says no to this spirit and yes to the Spirit of the Father. For this man of faith, there is a reality greater than self-centeredness—the invisible but real love of the Father. At this moment in the desert Jesus becomes the bearer of God's life-giving Spirit. Through him the Spirit shall become visible: "The blind see, the lame walk and the poor have the good news preached to them."

With Jesus' resurrection, his Spirit has been unleashed to live in the hearts of all those who believe in him. We now become the bearers of that life-giving Spirit. We have the capacity to love life into people if we choose, but like Jesus in the desert it means saying no to all the easy self-centered temptations.

For Personal Reflection

How and where is the Spirit of Jesus present in the world? Where is the Spirit of death present in the world?

Prayer to the Holy Spirit: "Come, Holy Spirit, fill the hearts of your faithful. Enkindle in us the fire of your love. Send forth your Spirit, and we shall be created, and you shall renew the face of the earth."

Questions for Review

1. Why does Jesus refer to God as "Abba"? How is this name different than Yahweh?

2. What does the word ''Messiah'' mean? Where did it originate? What were the Jewish people expecting of the Messiah? Why did Jesus avoid using the term ''Messiah'' to describe himself?

3. How did Jesus summarize the law and the Commandments? What role does the law play in the life of a Christian?

4. Why was Jesus so successful with ''sinners'' and why did he have such a difficult time with the scribes and Pharisees?

5. How does the scene of Jesus in the desert symbolize the struggle between life and death?

5

Key Events in the Life of Jesus

One of the most important characteristics of Jewish and Christian faith is the belief that God is encountered in history—in the events of peoples and individuals. Some religious traditions (especially in the East) tend to downplay the importance of history and emphasize the need to be free from the world in order to obtain true spiritual freedom. Although this has been a strand of thought among Christians throughout history, we believe that God is actively involved in the world and that events and people can reveal his presence.

God's revelation, however, is not limited to the big events of religious history—the exodus, the incarnation, the resurrection. God also reveals himself in and through "ordinary" lives. In the life of every human being, God is continuously and mysteriously at work. We may not think of it as the presence of God, but there are special people, places and events that deepen our lives, change their course and transform us as human beings. There are decisions that we make that lead us inexorably down one path and exclude us from walking other paths. The American poet Robert Frost recognized the presence of "key" moments and decisions that give shape to our identity:

Two roads diverged in a yellow wood,
And sorry I could not travel both

And be one traveller, long I stood
And looked down one as far as I could
To where it bent in the undergrowth;

Then took the other, as just as fair,
And having perhaps the better claim,
Because it was grassy and wanted wear;
Though as for that the passing there
Had worn them really about the same.

And both that morning equally lay
In leaves no step had trodden black.
Oh, I kept the first for another day!
Yet knowing how way leads on to way,
I doubted if I should ever come back.

I shall be telling this with a sigh
Somewhere ages and ages hence:
Two roads diverged in a wood, and I—
I took the one less travelled by,
And that has made all the difference.

For Personal Reflection

What have been the "key" events in your life thus far? How have they shaped your life?

When the writers of the Gospels told the story of Jesus, they often focused on the "key" events in his life. They represent the moments in Jesus' life that reveal most deeply who he was in relationship to the Father and to the world. In this chapter we will examine the meaning of seven such events: his birth, baptism, the temptations in the desert, the transfiguration, the Last Supper, his death and resurrection.

The Birth of Jesus

In the American society, our economy depends on the Christmas season. If Jesus had never been born, I'm sure we would invent another day of lavish gift-giving. At this time of the year the stores are transformed into madhouses of Christmas shoppers. Perhaps it is appropriate that it is the season for gifts because it is a celebration of the most unexpected, surprising and joy-filled gift to the universe—the gift of Love in person.

Christmas is a season of contrasts. It is very possibly the favorite and most celebrated day in the world. Yet it is also a time when loneliness is at its peak and the suicide rates climb. For those who are alone at Christmas time, their loneliness is heightened and their sense of emptiness is deepened. Yet at the midnight Mass we read that "the people who walked in darkness have seen a great light."

When Matthew and Luke tell their Christmas stories, they are working from different traditions, and, as we have seen, their stories emphasize different details. Usually, the Christmas story that we think of is a combination of two different stories.

Luke	**Matthew**
1. Birth of the Baptist	1. Joseph discovers Mary is pregnant
2. Angel appears to Mary	2. Angel appears to Joseph
3. Mary visits Elizabeth	3. Magi visit Jesus
4. The journey to Bethlehem	4. Herod slaughters the innocent boys
5. Birth in the stable accompanied by shepherds	5. Joseph, Mary and Jesus escape into Egypt
6. Jesus is circumcised	

Matthew and Luke tell different versions of the same event, but there is one important point that they agree on. Both of them say that Jesus is born of a virgin. The conception of the child is announced by an angel (in Matthew's Gospel the announcement is made to Joseph; in Luke's Gospel the announcement is made to Mary). The two Gospel writers are saying the same thing: the birth of Jesus is not another birth in the history of human births. Rather, in the birth of Jesus, God is at work in a unique and profound way. It is important to recognize that Mary's virginity is not supposed to mean that somehow sex is wrong and that God would never come into the world that way. It is a statement about Jesus that the Gospel writers are making, not a statement about sex. Jesus is *more* than the result of the natural biological union of a man and a woman. It is God at work. It is not something that could have been predicted or planned. It is not the natural culmination of human evolution. It is a gift beyond our wildest imaginations.

Yet in a sense the Christmas story is not only a story of what happened two thousand years ago, it is also a story of what continues to happen today. God's message still seeks out the person who is open to hearing it and capable of saying yes to it. Wise men still follow the light of the star in the midst of darkness. And evil, fearful men still seek to kill whatever threatens their power. Perhaps at this Christmas we should place our focus not only on the Christ Child born two thousand years ago, but on the Christ who waits to give birth in all mankind.

For Personal Reflection

1. What traditions does your family celebrate on Christmas? What do these traditions reflect about the meaning of Christmas? What can you do this year to put Christ in Christmas?

2. How is the virginal conception the "key" to the Christmas story?

The Baptism of Jesus

If you are a Catholic, the chances are good that you were baptized as a baby. Of course, you had no idea what was going on, but your parents were officially bringing you into the Church. Years later you can look back and see the significance of the baptism. It is possible that it was merely a social event and the christening party was the real highlight of the day. Or it is possible that the faith commitment that your parents have shared with you has developed into a faith commitment of your own. On the day of the baptism, however, you were certainly unaware of the importance of the event. It was not always this way in the Church. Originally when people were baptized in the Church, it meant a dramatic step in a new direction. Their lives had been changed by their faith in Christ, and their baptism was the visible sign of that change.

Jesus also received a baptism that gave direction to his life:

Jesus came from Nazareth in Galilee and was baptized in the Jordan by John. No sooner had he come up out of the water than he saw the heavens torn apart and the Spirit, like a dove, descending on him. And a voice came from the heavens: "You are my Son; my favor rests on you" (Mk 1:9–11).

In order to understand the meaning of the event, it is important to recognize that the baptism that Jesus receives is not the sacrament of baptism that we celebrate today that brings us into the Church. Those who were baptized by John did so as a sign of repentance for their sins. Because it was a baptism of repentance, it seemed inappropriate that Jesus would be baptized. In Matthew's version, John is aware of the problem: "John tried to dissuade him. 'It is I who need baptism from you,' he said, 'and yet you come to me.' But Jesus replied, 'Leave it like this for the time being; it is fitting that we should, in this way, do all that righteousness demands' '' (Mt 3:14–15). Jesus sees his baptism as part of the Father's plan for him. He takes on the baptism of sinners. He identifies himself with all those who are dependent on God's mercy.

Jesus' baptism represents the official beginning of his ministry, and his identification with those in need of repentance tells us a great deal about that ministry. It is at his baptism that Jesus says "yes" to the call of the Father, and we see the great extent of his authority: "You are my Son, the Beloved; my favor rests on you" (Mk 1:11).

For Personal Reflection

Jesus' baptism gave direction to his life. In what way has your baptism affected you? How would your life be different if you were not baptized?

The Temptations in the Desert

Have you ever noticed how so many of the great movies, books and plays have to do with the struggle between good and evil? These stories appeal to us because they are so true to our own experience of life and our own grappling with good and evil. Whether it is Luke Skywalker and Darth Vader or Macbeth and his conscience, the basic drama is the same—the human drama of good and evil.

In the Gospels we find the same drama being acted out. One reason why the Gospels continue to hold true from age to age is that they have a power to speak to the heart and experience of all peoples. The story of Jesus is the story of all mankind. In them we find the deepest questions of what it means to be a human being. In this sense the Gospels represent the great drama of God and man. It is in this light that we can better understand the story of the temptation of Jesus in the desert.

Any human being of modest intelligence or sensitivity is aware of the fact of evil. To deny the real presence of evil in the world would be as blind as denying the real presence of love and goodness. One need simply read a newspaper or examine one's conscience to confront it. In the story of the temptations, we are given an account of Jesus' personal confrontation with evil. In order to understand this account it is important that we do not read it as if it were a newspaper story interested in giving us the precise details of the conflict. This story of Jesus and Satan in the wilderness is not meant to be a literal account of a conversation that took place between Jesus and the devil. It is a form of dramatic literature designed to teach a truth about Jesus' life: like all of mankind Jesus must struggle with the forces of sin and evil and must say no to them in order to follow the will of the Father.

In these stories the Gospel writers present a clear picture of the human nature of Jesus. There is always a temptation on the part of Christians to "spiritualize" the humanity and personality of Jesus. We believe that he was human—but not really. After all, he was God underneath the human. The authors of the Synoptic Gospels do not support that type of thinking. Matthew, Mark and Luke all conclude the story of Jesus' baptism with the voice of the Father saying, "This is my beloved Son." They all seem very much aware of the divine status of Jesus, and yet they follow the story of the baptism with the story of the temptations in the desert. Jesus is tempted. He struggles with evil. This is not a make-believe struggle but a real one. When Jesus says "yes" to the Father, it has meaning because it is a real choice and not a programmed response. The human nature of Jesus is not simply a disguise that he wore. Jesus was fully human.

Matthew presents three temptations for Jesus: first, to turn stones into loaves: second, to leap from the top of the temple, and finally to bow down and worship Satan. What are these supposed to mean? A tipoff to their meaning can be found in their location. It was in the desert that the Jews had spent forty years after the exile in search of the promised land. During that time, they formed a covenant relationship with Yahweh. Yet they were continually unfaithful to Yahweh. The desert is the symbol of intense prayer, the place where one goes to confront oneself and one's God. Jesus, likewise, is tempted to be unfaithful to the Father. "Turn these stones into loaves," the tempter says to Jesus. Satan would rather that Jesus not focus on the Father but on the practical necessary ingredients for life. It is the very subtle temptation that we all face to take the easy way, not to make the sacrifices necessary to be a follower of Christ. Jesus is aware of a deeper need: "Man does not live on bread alone but on every word that comes from the mouth of God."

The second temptation finds Jesus in Jerusalem on top of the temple. Again the setting provides an important clue to the meaning. Jerusalem is the holy city and the temple is the very dwelling place of God. The temple represents the Jewish faith itself. Here Jesus is confronted with the type of religious leader that he will be. Satan says, "Throw yourself down and God will send his angels to catch you." Put on a show. Dazzle the crowd. Use the religion as a forum for your own greatness. Jesus replies, "You must not put the Lord your God to the test." God is not for show or spectacle or personal glory.

Finally, Jesus is brought out to a mountaintop to view all the kingdoms of the world and their splendor. They can be his. Will Jesus use his personality and intelligence for himself or for the Father? It is the most basic choice that he must make. Will he live for the kingdom of God or will he build his own kingdom? Jesus' response is: "You must love the Lord your God, and serve him alone."

In the temptations of Jesus, we are given another "key" by the Gospel authors. We are asked to recognize the humanity of Jesus for everything that it is—a humanity that must do battle with evil. Jesus is truly and fully one of us. The author of the Letter to the Hebrews describes it this way: "For it is not as though we had a high priest (Jesus) who was incapable of feeling our weaknesses with us; but we have one who was tempted in every way that we are, though he is without sin" (Heb 4:15). There is, however, another key to this story. Not only are we able to see the humanity of Jesus, but he reveals the meaning of our humanity. For Jesus, the meaning of life is found in his faithfulness to the will of the Father. Our temptations may be unique to our lives and yet they are basically the same ones that Jesus had to face. We want convenience and security. We try to manipulate God rather than serve him. We opt for power and glory in this life at the expense of God's kingdom. In a way, the story of Jesus' temptations is the story of our temptations. Perhaps more importantly, the story of his faithfulness may become the model of our conscience always seeking the loving thing to do.

For Personal Reflection

The Church has always taught that there is an evil in the world greater than any human evil. Evil is a power at work in the world. It is anti-love and anti-life. Traditionally we call this the devil. However, it is important not to overestimate the power of the devil. The battle between God and Satan is not an even match. The outcome is not in doubt. Christians can rest assured of the final victory over evil. However, it is possible for evil to triumph at times because of the human power not to choose love and life.

The Transfiguration (Mt 17:1–8)

I'll never forget the first time I climbed a mountain. I was with friends in the White Mountains of New Hampshire. The climb was very steep and I had to stop frequently to catch my breath. I wondered what I had gotten myself into. The climb was not very exciting. All that lay in front of me was a steep path, and I trudged along for hours. Suddenly we were on the ridge of the mountain overlooking the Presidential Range. It was so spectacular and gorgeous that it took my breath away. We stopped on the ridge to have lunch. I was in awe the whole time. When it was time to move on, I pleaded that we remain a little longer, but my request was denied. It was back to trudging along the path up the mountain. But now there was a difference. Now I had a vision of what lay ahead.

In the Bible and in other religious literature, the mountain is often a symbol of the meeting place between God and man. It is on Mount Sinai that Moses receives the law, the Ten Commandments. It is on the mountain that Matthew situates the great sermon of Jesus. It is also on the mountain that Jesus is transfigured before Peter, James and John. It is a rather strange and mystical story. The clothing of Jesus glows. Moses and Elijah appear and then disappear. What does the story mean?

The transfiguration takes place immediately after Jesus has recognized the fact that he will go to Jerusalem but that he will not be triumphant. In Jerusalem he must suffer and die. His insistence on telling the truth has brought him into direct conflict with the leaders of the Jewish faith. A group of them have become convinced that he is a false prophet and a menace to Israel and the law of Moses. He will have to pay the price. Jesus has realized that he may have to die if he remains true to the will of the Father. He is willing to suffer the consequences, and it is on the mountaintop that he is given a glimpse of the glory that lies beyond the suffering. His suffering and death will not be in vain. In fact, they will become the instruments through which he is glorified in the resurrection. In a way, the transfiguration was like my experience on the ridge of the mountain. It is a "pre-view" of the view from the top, an insight into the great things yet to come. I did not want to leave the ridge. Peter does not want to leave the mountaintop: "Lord, it is good for us to be here. If you wish I will make three tents here" (Mt 17:4). But they must go down the mountain to the "real" world. However, they all resume the trip to Jerusalem with a vision and hope for the journey ahead.

This type of experience is not unique to the apostles. Many great Christians have had the experience of being caught up in the presence and glory of God. These experiences become for them the inspiration for their work. Martin Luther King was one Christian who liked to employ the symbolism of the mountaintop in describing the black man's quest for freedom. For King, it was not a trip to Jerusalem but a trip to Memphis that he had to endure. Like Jesus, he had to remain faithful to the will of God as he understood it. He had to be faithful to the truth no matter what the consequences. As Jesus walked down the mountain with the apostles, about to begin his fateful trip to Jerusalem, his thoughts may have been similar to Dr. King's on the night before his death:

> We've got some difficult days ahead. But it doesn't matter with me now. Because I've been to the mountaintop. And I don't mind. Like anyone I would like to live a long life. Longevity has its place. But I'm not concerned about that now. I just want to do God's will. And He's allowed me to go up to the mountain. And I've looked over. And I've seen the promised land. I may not get there with you. But I want you to know tonight, that we, as a people, will get to the promised land. And I'm happy tonight. I'm not worried about anything. I'm not fearing any man. Mine eyes have seen the glory of the coming of the Lord.

For Personal Reflection

Abraham Maslow, a great American psychologist, described certain moments in life as "peak experiences." According to

Maslow, people who make full use of their potential experience moments when they feel deeply alive and sensitive to all of life. In peak experiences, there is a heightened sense of justice, wholeness, richness, simplicity, beauty, goodness, honesty, playfulness and independence. We cannot experience this richness in life unless there is a certain "dying to oneself," a lack of self-centeredness and a willingness to make the sacrifices necessary for love and truth (see *Toward a Psychology of Being,* Van Nostrand Reinhold Company, New York, 1968). Translated into these psychological terms, the transfiguration certainly represents a "peak experience" for Jesus.

Have you ever experienced a "peak moment"? Carefully recall the experience. How can you live that way more often?

The Last Supper

Dinnertime, in most homes, is a time for more than eating. It is a time for the family to be together. It is a time for communication. The next time your family has dinner together, watch the channels of communication and the various messages that take place at the table. You may be able to discover some interesting dynamics taking place. Your father, for example, may have a certain tone of voice that alerts you to a mood he is in. Your mother may be able to say more in one look than in ten sentences. You may not say anything at all—and that says something. Meals have been used traditionally to do more than simply fill bellies. Meals are a central part of many celebrations and parties. They are community builders. They have also been at the center of Jewish and Christian ritual for thousands of years.

There is one meal in particular that occupies a place of special importance in the Jewish heritage. It is the seder meal—the meal that celebrates the Passover feast. The key event in the history of Israel was the exodus, the escape from slavery in Egypt.

Every year the Jewish people would recall this great event in the celebration of the Passover. All the details of the seder meal were meant to help the Jewish people relive this solemn event. They dressed as a people in flight. They ate bitter herbs to remind themselves of the bitterness of the desert. They ate lamb to recall the blood of the lamb smeared on their doorposts to save them from the angel of death. They ate unleavened bread, the "bread of affliction" that had to be baked in haste, for they were a people in flight. Each year God's great act of salvation would be recalled and relived in this seder meal. The covenant between God and his people would be renewed.

On the night before his death, Jesus used this meal to try to communicate to his disciples the meaning of his life and death. During the course of the meal, Jesus changed its meaning. No longer was the bread to recall the flight from Egypt, but instead: "This is my body which will be given for you; do this as a memorial of me" (Lk 22:19). The cup of wine is no longer a celebration of the old covenant, but rather, "This cup is the new covenant in my blood which will be poured out for you" (Lk 22:20). No longer are the apostles to celebrate the exodus as the great act of salvation. It has been fulfilled in Jesus. Jesus is the bread broken and the wine poured out. He is the great saving act of God. Jesus is not simply saying goodbye to his friends. What he did and said that evening would be continued as long as Christians continued to come together. The Last Supper had a universal meaning to it. No longer does salvation come from the blood of the lamb but from the blood of Christ. No longer is the covenant established through the law of Moses; now the new covenant comes from faith in Jesus. No longer does this ritual meal recall the exodus, but, as Jesus said, "Do this as a memorial of me."

For Personal Reflection

The Eucharist is at the center of Christian faith. Through it
Christ continues to be present to us in a special way. What does
the Mass mean to you at this stage of your life? Do you go there
with the attitude of the Christian (giving of yourself) or do you go
there with a childish attitude (what's in it for me)?

Jesus' Death

Perhaps there is no event in the life of Jesus quite as difficult
to understand as his death. There are many questions that surround
this issue. Why does Jesus go to Jerusalem if he knows that he
will be killed? Why is Jesus put to death? What do we mean when
we say that Jesus' death saves us? Why does God allow his own
Son to be treated so badly?

The central Christian symbol is the cross. It seems odd that
we put our faith in a man who was executed by the Roman authorities and died a rather obscure death outside the city of Jerusalem. Yet Christians believe that this death was also a divine act
of salvation. The meaning of this can only be understood in the
context of Jesus' life. The fact that Jesus would die should be no
surprise to anyone. Death is a fact of human existence. The minute
any one of us is born, we begin moving inexorably toward death.
Because Jesus is truly human, he will not be an exception to this
reality. But the important thing about Jesus' death is not the fact
that he dies but the meaning of his death. Death puts us face to
face with the question: "What is the meaning of life?" We are
forced to ask ourselves whether or not there is any ultimate purpose to our life on earth. When the death is brutal and tortuous,
the question is all the more obvious. What's the point?

When it is time for Jesus to die, he faces it with nothing less
than dread. He does not want to die. He is still young. He is in-

nocent of any wrongdoing. Death by Roman execution is cruci-
fixion—a long and agonizing process meant to deter criminals.
Mark relays the story of Jesus facing death in no uncertain terms:

> They came to a small estate called Gethsemane, and Jesus
> said to his disciples, "Stay here while I pray." Then he took
> Peter and James and John with him. And a sudden fear came
> over him, and great distress. And he said to them, "My soul
> is sorrowful to the point of death. Wait here and keep
> awake." And going on a little further, he threw himself on
> the ground and prayed that, if it were possible, this hour
> might pass him by. "Abba (Father)," he said. "Everything
> is possible for you. Take this cup away from me. But let it be
> as you, not I would have it" (Mk 14:32–36).

Here is the key to the meaning of Jesus' death: absolute trust
in the Father. Jesus' entire life has been lived on this faith and
trust. He will face death with the same faith. For Jesus there is
something worse than death and that is to be untrue to the meaning
of his life.

Traditionally, Christians have always believed that Jesus'
death has a meaning far greater than the death of any other person.
Jesus' death (and resurrection) saves us from sin. What do we
mean by this? One way that the question has been answered is to
say that Jesus' death reopened the gates of heaven. God had closed
heaven because of mankind's sins and would not reopen it until
he received the perfect sacrifice. Since no one was capable of this,
he sent his own Son to suffer and die. This is a very poor explanation of salvation. A God who desires the suffering and death of
his own Son is out of character with the loving Father revealed by
Jesus. Jesus' death saves us because it reveals the depth of God's
love for us. The love that Jesus showed in dying on the cross is
the mirror image of God's love for us. It is a love that is total and
unconditional. Jesus' death also reveals that there is nothing, not

even death, that can stand between us and God's love. St. Paul describes it this way in his Letter to the Romans:

> With God on our side who can be against us? . . . Nothing therefore can come between us and the love of Christ. . . . For I am certain of this: neither death nor life, no angel, no prince, nothing that exists or is yet to come, not any power or height or depth, nor any created thing can come between us and the love of God made visible in Christ Jesus our Lord (Rom 8:31, 35, 38–39).

The cross of Christ remains for the Christian today a sign of the way to the Father. On the one hand the cross reveals that love and self-surrender are the only way to the Father. On another level, however, the cross remains a constant reminder of the fact of evil and selfishness in the world. Wherever persons are oppressed, human dignity or needs are denied, or justice and love are unwelcomed, Christ continues to be crucified in the world. The cross remains a glaring reminder that the kingdom has not yet come in its fullness, and that the cost of being a disciple can be a very high one.

For Personal Reflection

Death is part of our common human experience. Sickness, separation from a loved one, divorce, the death of a friend or relative, loneliness and depression are all forms of dying. These experiences can help teach us that death is not the end and that future growth and happiness are possible. What has your experience of death been like? How have you responded to those situations?

The Resurrection

Everything that has been said here about Jesus' death presumes the resurrection. The resurrection is God's reply that death is not the final word. It is not the ultimate winner.

But just what was the resurrection? What happened and how did it happen? Unfortunately, these are questions that are impossible to answer because there were no direct witnesses of the event. The evidence begins with an empty tomb where the body of Jesus had been laid. However, it is possible to draw certain conclusions from the written testimony concerning the resurrection. To begin with, resurrection is different than resuscitation. Resuscitation is the revival of an apparently dead body. There are people who wrote books about being clinically dead and then returning to life. These would be examples of resuscitation. Sooner or later these people will have to die. Resurrection, however, is more than being brought back to life. It is moving into a whole new dimension of existence. When we read the stories about Jesus' resurrection, this becomes obvious. Mary, his friend, does not recognize him and then is warned not to touch him (Jn 20). It is the same Jesus and yet he is radically changed. The disciples who meet him on the road to Emmaus do not know him until the breaking of the bread (Lk 24). At another time, Jesus simply appears in a room without any need to open the door (Jn 20). Jesus is no longer limited by normal human limitations. He is no longer bound by categories of space and time. He can be in more than one place at one time.

The resurrection is *the* key experience in the life of Jesus. As St. Paul would write later on: "If Christ has not been raised you are still in your sins" (1 Cor 15:17). The basis of everything that Christians believe about Jesus rests on the resurrection. According to Peter, it is at the resurrection that Jesus is finally revealed as Lord and Christ. Until the resurrection, the disciples never fully comprehended the meaning of Jesus' life and death. It is only at the resurrection that they are able to make the great proclamation of faith: Jesus is Lord (see Acts 2:22–25, 36).

In fact the cross and resurrection must be seen as one event because they are inseparable. If the cross is the symbol of loving self-surrender, the resurrection is the fruit and joy of that love. If the cross is the sign of the ongoing struggle with evil, the resurrection is our hope and guarantee in that struggle. St. Paul was aware of the dynamic of cross and resurrection when he wrote: "I think that what we suffer in this life can never be compared to the glory as yet unrevealed which is waiting for us. . . . From the beginning until now the entire creation, as we know, has been groaning in one great act of giving birth" (Rom 8:18, 22). The resurrection of Jesus reveals not only the meaning of Jesus' life but the meaning of all creation. The world and its people have been created to share in the glory of the Father. What is the meaning of Jesus' life? What is the meaning of your life? What is the destiny of human history? In a word, the resurrection.

For Personal Reflection

Christians do not talk about the resurrection as much as about "going to heaven." Are they the same thing? What are some common notions of heaven? Stretching your imagination, what are some qualities that you would associate with resurrected life? (In other words, what will heaven be like in your best dreams?)

Questions for Review

1. What is the significance of Mary's virginity? What does it tell us about Jesus?

2. What does Jesus' baptism mean to him? Why does he allow John to baptize him?

3. What are the three temptations offered to Jesus in the desert and what do they symbolize?

4. What is the relationship between the Last Supper and the Passover? How does Jesus change the meaning of the Passover meal?

5. What do we mean when we say that Jesus' death saves us?

6. In what way is the cross a symbol of God's love and the reality of evil?

7. What is the difference between resuscitation and resurrection? How is Jesus different after his resurrection?

6

Parables and the Kingdom

In examining the Gospels, we have seen how each evangelist portrayed the person of Jesus and emphasized different aspects of his personality. We have also examined the "key" events in the life of Jesus and the meaning of those events. In this chapter we would like to look closely at the teaching and preaching of Jesus. What was the core of Jesus' message? What relevance does that teaching have for us today?

For Personal Reflection

If you met someone who had never heard of Jesus Christ, how would you summarize his message and teaching?

How did you answer the reflection above? The most common answer to that question is that Jesus told us to love one another. It's hard to argue with that because love certainly was central to the good news. However, the main theme of Jesus' teaching is actually the kingdom of God. This includes his teaching on love, but it is not as simple as that. What is the kingdom of God? Jesus never really spells it out as such. Instead he tells stories about the kingdom, and from these stories we can get an insight into what this kingdom is all about.

The Parables

We have already seen that the Gospels do not give us the exact words of Jesus at all times. Much of what is in the Gospels reflects not only the words of Christ but their interpretation by the early Church. It can be difficult to discern what is from Christ and what is not. There is, however, one part of the Gospels that the scholars believe is directly traceable to the teaching of Jesus. These are the parables. These stories that Jesus used to teach are unique to him, and therefore we can be confident that when we listen to the parables we are very close to the words of Jesus. This is not to say that the Church did not change or adapt them in some circumstances. They did use the parables as teaching instruments for their own communities and may have added their own conclusion to a parable to fit their own circumstances. However the fact remains that the parables are the best place to uncover the teaching and message of Jesus.

Before we examine some of the themes in the parables, we should first clarify what it is that we are talking about. Jesus was a great storyteller. He told stories that captured the attention and the imagination of his listeners. However, his stories were meant to be more than amusements. In the midst of the parables are the secrets to the kingdom of God. These stories are called parables, from the Greek *parabole,* meaning a comparison of two things. Jesus would use the everyday events and circumstances of life and compare them to the kingdom of God. The parables of Jesus are unique. There is nothing else quite like them in the Bible. There are four main characteristics to a parable that can help us to understand them.

1. Parables use facts and details that are true to life (as opposed to fables in which there are talking animals, magic potions etc.).

2. There is one main point to a parable. There are not many hidden or symbolic meanings.
3. The parables of Jesus are told in a certain setting and to specific people. They are not "pearls of wisdom" delivered for their own sake (like the proverbs or the sayings of Ben Franklin).
4. Parables very often have a surprise or a "twist" at the end of the story to shock the reader into thinking a new way.

The parables are Jesus' way of describing the kingdom. He does not use a philosophical theory, nor does he set up a systematic theology. Instead he tells stories that he knows the people can relate to. Behind those stories, however, is a call to a new kind of life. Let's look at five different aspects of the kingdom of God that we find revealed in the parables.

I The Time Has Come

What time is it?
Nine o'clock! Oh God, I overslept!
Friday, 3 P.M. Finally.
The day before the term paper is due. The time has come.
Time is not simply the passing of minutes, days and hours. Time has a personality of its own. There is nighttime and daytime, dawn and dusk, morning, afternoon and evening. There are times of rejoicing and celebrating, times of mourning and sadness, times of death and rebirth. If you examine your own life, you may notice that there are times when the days are little more than eating and sleeping. There is nothing very significant about these days. But there are other times that are special: celebrating Christmas, making a new friend, falling in love, playing in a big game, getting the part in the play. These times are special because they are filled with meaning. Life seems more intensified. They need not necessarily be good times either. Times of sickness, suffering and death can be intensified experiences of life.

In Greek there are two words for "time": *chronos* and *kairos*. *Chronos* refers to the simple passage of time. (We get "chronology" from this word.) *Kairos,* on the other hand, is special time—time in which life is intensified and filled with meaning. In the Old Testament, *kairos* is the time of judgment and salvation. The Jewish people waited in hope for the day of Yahweh (*kairos*) when the kingdom of God would be established. On that day, "the lion and the lamb will lie down." Peace would be established. The world would reflect the Lordship of God over all things. Salvation history, the creation itself, the patriarchs, Moses, David, Solomon, the prophets—all point to this time of fulfillment in which God will complete his purposes and establish his reign.

From the mouth of Jesus we hear the message, "The time has come and the kingdom of God is close at hand. Repent and believe the good news" (Mk 1:15). The message of Jesus is primarily one of fulfillment and urgency. All that has been awaited and hoped for is here! Don't miss out! This theme of being alert to the special time is a theme of some of Jesus' parables. There is a brief parable in Matthew and Luke that develops this theme:

> What description can I find for this generation? It is like children shouting to each other as they sit in the marketplace:

> "We played the pipes for you,
> and you wouldn't dance;
> we sang dirges,
> and you wouldn't be mourners" (Mt 11:16–17).

What does this parable mean? Jesus is warning his listeners to pay attention. The hand of God is among you and you are missing it because you are like children in the marketplace shouting and playing with each other and oblivious to what is going on around them. John the Baptist began the fulfillment with a message of God's impending judgment ("we sang dirges for you").

Jesus, on the other hand, emphasized God's love and mercy and the good news of salvation (''we played the pipes for you''). In both cases the Jewish leaders are not responding. They claim that the Baptist was possessed and that Jesus is a glutton and a drunkard. Wake up! The time is here!

We also find this theme evident in the parable of the great supper:

> There was a man who gave a great banquet, and he invited a large number of people. When the time for the banquet came, he sent his servant to say to those who had been invited, ''Come along, everything is ready now.'' But all alike started to make excuses. The first said, ''I have bought a piece of land and must go and see it. Please accept my apologies.'' Another said, ''I have bought five yoke of oxen and am on my way to try them out. Please accept my apologies.'' Yet another said, ''I just got married and so am unable to come.''
>
> The servant returned and reported this to his master. Then the householder, in a rage, said to the servant, ''Go out quickly into the streets and the alleys of the town and bring in here the poor, the crippled, the blind and the lame.'' ''Sir,'' said the servant, ''your orders have been carried out and there is still room.'' Then the master said to his servant, ''Go to the open rows and the hedgerows and force people to come in to make sure my house is full; because I tell you not one of those invited shall have a taste of my banquet'' (Mt 14:15–24).

In this parable and in much of Jewish literature, God's salvation is depicted as a banquet. But the leaders of Judaism are declining the invitation to the feast. The party is being thrown and they are refusing to participate. When Jesus originally told this parable, it was probably meant to explain his association with the sinners and tax collectors. The reason: the fulfillment is now! If the scribes and the Pharisees will not respond, the banquet will be held for those who will come.

For Personal Reflection

One of the biggest mistakes that people make is living in the future or the past instead of the present: "When I graduate things will be different" or "Things were different back in my day." Psychologists say that one of the main ingredients in happiness is our ability to live in the present. Jesus, as usual, was many years ahead of his time. He challenged people to be alert to the signs of God's presence in their midst. Where are you living? In the present building a future or imagining a future and missing the here and now?

𝕀 The Hidden, Mysterious Power of God

> He went on to say, "What is the kingdom of God like? What shall I compare it with? It is like a mustard seed which a man took and threw into his garden; it grew and became a tree and the birds of the air sheltered in its branches."
>
> Another thing he said, "What shall I compare the kingdom of God with? It is like the yeast a woman took and mixed in with three measures of flour till it was leavened all through" (Lk 13:18–21).

These two parables are typical of Jesus' stories about the kingdom. Jesus uses images that the people are familiar with from their daily life; the image of a woman baking bread and the image of a mustard seed and tree. But what do these images tell us about the kingdom? What is the connection between the kingdom and yeast and mustard seeds? There are two important elements to these parables. First, like the yeast and the mustard seed, God's presence and power in the world is hidden and mysterious. The world that we live in tends to measure people and things by external standards. Good looks, wealth, a sense of humor and success are often the standards that we use to judge. Not so in the kingdom. What is valuable in the kingdom cannot be seen but through the eyes of faith and love. The kingdom lives in the heart and soul. It is an invisible and spiritual quality that remains hidden to those who judge only with the normal standards that the world uses.

The second point behind these parables is the miraculous disproportion between the yeast and the leavened bread and the seed and the tree. A tiny bit of yeast has had an incredible effect on the flour. The tiny mustard seed grows into a tree. Although the kingdom is a hidden reality its power is extraordinary. The effects of God's activity are miraculous. Perhaps there is no better example of this than the person Jesus. Here was a man born to poor parents in an obscure town in a remote country far from the great center of the world, Rome. He was a carpenter turned preacher. He was put to death by the Roman authorities as a threat to the well-being of the state. He wrote no books. He had no great formal education. He died a terrible death. And yet no one in the history of mankind has had the effect on this planet that he has had. Jesus himself is like the seed and the yeast that he speaks of. God makes great things happen that by all other measures would seem impossible.

For Personal Reflection

1. Think of some examples when little things meant a lot.
2. Make a resolution to do some "little things" for your family and friends (and maybe even enemies).

The Kingdom Is a Gift

People who are involved in religion as a profession (as I am) should always remember one thing: the people that Jesus had the most difficulty with were people like us. The problem that "religious" people run into is that there is always a tendency to think that you are doing God some great big favor, and concluding: "Now he owes me." Many of the religious leaders of Jesus' day felt this way, and it seemed to drive Jesus crazy. These people felt that they could earn their way into the kingdom with good deeds and obedience to the law. Some seemed to feel that they should have a special status above other people because of their religious life. This certainly wasn't a part of Jesus' teaching. For Jesus, the love of God was a gift infinitely greater than any of us could earn. A life of virtue is great, but it doesn't earn us a special place with God. God's love for us is like the love of a mother for her baby. The child cries in the middle of the night and the mother continues to love it. She can act no other way. Such is God's love for us. In order to describe the great gift and generosity of God's love, Jesus told the story of the laborers in the vineyard:

Now the kingdom of God is like a landowner going out at daybreak to hire workers for his vineyard. He made an agreement with the workers for one denarius a day, and sent them to his vineyard. Going out at about the third hour he saw others standing idly in the marketplace and said to them. "You go to my vineyard too and I will give you a fair wage." So they went. At the sixth hour and at about the ninth hour, he went out and did the same. Then at about the eleventh hour he went out and found more men standing around, and he said to them, "Why have you been standing here idle all day?" "Because no one has hired us," they answered. He said to them, "You go into my vineyard too." In the evening, the owner of the vineyard said to his bailiff, "Call the workers and pay them their wages, starting with the last arrivals and ending with the first." So those who were hired at the eleventh hour came forward and received one denarius each. When the first came, they expected to get more, but they too received one denarius each. They took it, but grumbled at the

landowner. "The men who came last," they said, "have
done only one hour, and you have treated them the same as
us, though we have done a heavy day's work in all the heat."
He answered one of them and said, "My friend, I am not
being unjust to you; did we not agree on one denarius? Take
your earnings and go. I choose to pay the last comer as much
as I pay you. Have I no right to do what I like with my own?
Why be envious because I am generous?" (Mt 20:1–15).

In order to understand this parable it helps to put ourselves
back into the time of Jesus. In those days men looking for work
went into the marketplace where they waited for someone to hire
them. Those hired late in the day would have little to show for
their work on returning home and so the owner in this parable pays
them a full day's wages. Meanwhile those who had worked much
longer grumbled about this injustice. They should receive more
than the others. It was simply a question of being fair.

It is important to remember not to take the story at face value.
Jesus is not telling landowners how to run their businesses. He is
trying to talk about the kingdom of God. The parable was probably addressed originally to the self-righteous Pharisees who were
upset at Jesus for proclaiming the good news to sinners. What had
they done to earn God's love? Had not they, the religious leaders,
worked long and hard for God? Had not they earned more of
God's reward? This type of small-mindedness was completely
missing the point: God's love is a gift not to be hoarded but for
all to rejoice in.

For Personal Reflection

Reread the story of the laborers in the vineyard and answer
this question: Is God fair?

℣ In God's Kingdom There Is Reconciliation and Forgiveness

Perhaps one of the most important things to remember about the kingdom of God is that it was not meant to be something that occurred only in the future. Essential to Jesus' message was the belief that the kingdom had begun *now*. Essential to this kingdom was reconciliation. We have already seen many times how Jesus was the champion of mercy and forgiveness. It should not be surprising that his most famous parable was centered around this theme. It is called the parable of the prodigal son but is probably better named the parable of the loving father because it is the father who is really the central character (see Lk 15:11–32).

Like many of Jesus' parables, this one is best understood when we try to place ourselves into the mindset of Jesus' listeners. The first important thing to recognize in this parable is the nature of the boy's insult to his father. The boy wants his share of the inheritance now. Maybe you should try this with your father. Ask him if you are included in the will, and, if so, if you can have your inheritance today. It is like saying, "Hey, dad, I can't wait for you to die." The boy is a self-centered ingrate. And yet the father does not try to coerce his love.

The boy goes his own way spending the money on wine, women and song. However, his money runs out and there is a famine in the country that has reduced him to feeding pigs. Always being one to look after his own best interests, he decides that he will go back home, plead for mercy and ask to be taken on as a slave at his father's house. He begins the journey home.

One day, as the father looked off into the distance, he saw the boy still a long way off. He ran to greet him. Now in those days, Jewish elders never ran. It was considered to be undignified for a man of his position. But the father would save his dignity for another day—his son had returned! The boy's well-rehearsed story is cut short. The father will not hear of requests to be a servant. He had never ceased being his father, so the boy could never stop being his son. It was time to celebrate! What had been broken was now restored.

But the story is not over. There is another son, one who has been faithful and worked hard for many years. When he hears that his father is throwing a party for his selfish brother, he is furious! He goes into the house and begins an argument with his father. "All these years I have slaved for you!" He does not seem to understand. The father is not looking for slaves. He delights in the happy return of his children. The older son shares in the attitude of many of those listening to the parable: he resents the mercy of God being shown to those who have strayed from the law. They did not have the compassion needed to welcome back a lost brother.

For Personal Reflection

The theme of this parable is present in many books, plays and movies. Can you think of any that reflects this theme of conflict and reconciliation?

ⅴ The Kingdom Calls for a Commitment

Much of what has been said so far emphasizes God's love, forgiveness and unbounded generosity. However, there is another side to this coin. There is our response to God's gift. Those who have been touched by the love of God must become sharers of that love with others. Faith must become for us a way of life, a commitment that we live from day to day. Christ never in his wildest dreams imagined faith as something that we give for an hour on Sunday. Rather, the faith commitment was one that would color the way that we did everything. Our faith is something that needs to be given a strong priority in our life. If we fail to live it, we can lose it. Two parables illustrate the point:

> The kingdom of heaven is like a treasure hidden in a field which someone has found; he hides it again, goes off happy, sells everything that he owns and buys the field.
>
> Again, the kingdom of heaven is like a merchant looking for fine pearls; when he finds one of great value he goes and sells everything that he owns and buys it (Mt 13:44-45).

Again, we must remember we are not being given real estate or business advice. Jesus is talking about the kingdom. What is the comparison? It is the willingness of these men to give up other things in order to have what they treasure the most. The same is true of the kingdom. What is needed is commitment. In these parables, Jesus challenges our priorities in life. The qualities of the kingdom, faith, love, mercy, peace, and trust, must be more important than anything else.

For Personal Reflection

1. What are your priorities in life? How would you rank the following in order of importance:

good looks	sense of humor	a good job
popularity	good friends	having a boy/girl friend
good family	peace in the world	intelligence
athletic ability	wealth	faith

2. When you were baptized, your parents made a commitment to raise you in the Church. Ultimately, however, the choice of faith will belong to you. Where are you in making the faith commitment your own choice?

No faith			Thinking it over				I believe!		
1	2	3	4	5	6	7	8	9	10

Questions for Review

1. What are four main characteristics of a parable?

2. What are two Greek words for ''time''? How are they different and how does one relate to the message of Jesus?

3. In what way can a mustard seed and leaven be compared to the kingdom of God?

4. To whom is Jesus addressing the parable of the laborers in the vineyard? What is the main point of the parable?

5. Why is the parable of the prodigal son better named the parable of the loving father? Whom does the older son in this story represent?

6. What two parables of Jesus emphasize the importance of commitment?

7

The Gospel of John

We now turn our attention to the one Gospel that is different from the others: the Gospel of John. Even a quick glance at this Gospel will reveal that it is quite unique in its style and in its theme. Before we look at the Gospel itself, let us list some of the differences to look for:

1. John's Gospel is more symbolic than the Synoptic Gospels. Throughout his Gospel John uses key symbols to teach about the meaning of Jesus. These symbols include the Word, life, light and darkness, the bread of life, the hour, glory, and signs.

2. In John's Gospel, Jesus often speaks in long philosophical/theological discourses. In the Synoptics, Jesus' language is much more direct.

3. There are no parables in John's Gospel.

4. Jesus rarely mentions the kingdom of God. Instead, he talks mostly about himself or about eternal life.

5. There are fewer miracles in John's Gospel. He lists only seven, and he calls them "signs."

6. John has a different sequence of events. In his Gospel, he mentions three trips to Jerusalem. The Synoptics mention only one.

7. John emphasizes the divine nature of Jesus. The Synoptics seem to give a more balanced picture of Jesus' human and divine natures.

In order to try to capture the unique nature of John's Gospel, we will examine some of the images that he uses to describe Jesus. We will then briefly look at John's insight into the call to follow Jesus.

Jesus, the Word

It is difficult for us to imagine how hard it must have been for Jesus' followers to come to the recognition that he was God. We have grown up with this idea from the moment that we heard of Jesus, but it was exactly the opposite for the Jews of Jesus' time. It was difficult to imagine that the Messiah could possibly be a carpenter's son from Nazareth. It was unthinkable that the Messiah would be God himself. The idea that a man would be God was as foreign to the Jews as the knowledge of modern science. Yet this was what Jesus' followers were affirming. After the resurrection, it becomes clear to them for the first time that Jesus is God's equal.

The Synoptic Gospels make it clear that Jesus was the Son of God even before the resurrection. Mark's Gospel includes the scene at the baptism of Jesus in which the Father says. "This is my beloved Son." Matthew and Luke, in their infancy narratives, make it clear that Jesus is the Son of God from the moment of his conception and birth. John develops the idea that has become a mainstay of Christian theology ever since: Jesus is the pre-existent Son of God. Even before his birth, Jesus existed with the Father and then became a human being. We find this idea developed in the Prologue to John's Gospel.

> In the beginning was the Word:
> the Word was with God
> and the Word was God.
> He was with God in the beginning.
> Through him all things came to be,
> not one thing had its being but through him.
> All that came to be had life in him
> and that life was the light of men,
> a light that shines in the dark,
> a light that darkness could not overpower. . . .
> The Word was made flesh;
> he lived among us,
> and we saw his glory,
> the glory that is his as the only Son of the Father,
> full of grace and truth (Jn 1:1–5, 14).

John's Gospel begins with this hymn. As you can see the style and content are very different from the Synoptic Gospels. John refers to Jesus as the Word, a title that we find mentioned at no other time in the New Testament. What is he trying to tell us about Jesus?

Words can have a great deal of power to them. Great preachers use words to inspire their congregations. Politicians use words to persuade people to vote for them. The great ideas of history are passed from one generation to the next by words. Words can also be used to reveal ourselves. There are times that we need to talk— to get things off our chest. These words can help put us at peace with ourselves. There are also times when a carefully chosen word can make someone's day. The words we use express who we are. It is in this sense that John describes Jesus as the Word. Jesus is God's communication of himself.

John begins the Prologue with the same three words that begin the Bible: "In the beginning." This is certainly no coincidence. John's point is to show that the Word of God existed from the beginning of time. However, this is not the main point. The climax of the Prologue comes in verse 14: "The Word was made flesh; he lived among us." From the beginning of his Gospel, John has given us the heart of his theology: Jesus is God in person! God has achieved the ultimate in communication to his people. He has spoken his Word in Christ. He has become flesh and blood.

When we say to someone, "I give you my word," we are putting our very selves on the line. In Jesus, God has given us his Word.

For Personal Reflection

Can you think of a time in your life when someone's words meant a great deal to you?

Jesus, the Light of the World

When I was a little kid, I used to share a room with my two brothers. Peter, the oldest of the three, demanded that the lights be out and the door shut when we went to bed. Phil and I would have no part of this. We wanted the hall light left on and the door open. Why were we afraid of the dark? Logically, there was nothing to fear. We lived in a safe neighborhood. But logic meant little to two small boys. The fact is that darkness seems to be a universal symbol for insecurity and fear. Carl Jung, a psychologist who did much of his work studying the unconscious, believed that there were such things as archetypal symbols. These are symbols that are embedded in the unconscious of everyone. Darkness is one of these symbols. It represents confusion, fear and insecurity. The light, on the other hand, represents trust, security and truth. The

Bible often uses these symbols to represent good and evil, creativity and confusion. We need look no further than the first creation account in Genesis:

> In the beginning God created the heavens and the earth. Now the earth was a formless void, there was darkness over the deep, and God's spirit hovered over the water.
>
> God said, "Let there be light," and there was light. God saw that light was good, and God divided light from darkness (Gen 1:1–4).

Later Isaiah delivers a message of hope to the Jewish people using the same symbols. It is the passage that we read at Christmas:

> The people that walked in darkness
> has seen a great light;
> on those who lived in a land of deep shadow
> a light has shone (Is 9:1).

In John's Gospel, Jesus identifies himself with the light:

> "I am the light of the world;
> anyone who follows me
> will not be walking in the dark;
> he will have the light of life" (Jn 8:12).

Jesus is the one who enables us to see life as it really is. In a world filled with darkness, to follow Christ means to walk in the light. Those who have the light can see. They have more than sight, they have insight. They recognize life's meaning.

For Personal Reflection

Blindfold a friend and lead him or her around by the hand. Reverse roles and go to as many places as possible. Perhaps this little experiment will help you get a better sense of the symbolism of light and darkness.

Jesus, the Way, the Truth and the Life

Jesus said,

I am the Way, the Truth and the Life.
No one can come to the Father except through me.
If you know me, you know my Father too.
From this moment you have known him and have seen him (Jn 14:6–7).

In John's Gospel (and nowhere else in the New Testament), Jesus refers to himself as the Way. In order to appreciate this title better, it may help to know that before the followers of Jesus were called Christians, they were known as followers of the Way. Christianity's original name was simply "the Way." Of course, the way that Christians were supposed to live was the way of Jesus. He provided the direction to their life. This notion of the way also emphasizes the moral demands of Christianity. For Christians there is a way to act and a way not to act. That way is the way of love. Thus, the distinguishing characteristic of the Church is summed up in the statement, "These Christians, see how they love one another."

There is one final connection that we should make with "the Way." This title emphasizes the fact that our relationship with Christ is an ongoing process. The life of faith is a journey. Like any journey, it will include its peaks and valleys. It will include both struggle and joy. Christians are people who are "on the way." They have not yet arrived. Some people see their faith as providing the answer to every question in life. This is not true for the Christian who walks life's journey, often very aware that he has not yet arrived, but he remains faithful to walking in the way of Jesus.

For Personal Reflection

Do you think of faith as a set of beliefs or as a way of life? Which of the following words do you associate with faith?

certainty or searching	going to church or helping the poor
God or man	suffering or joy
conviction or indecision	gift or accomplishment
prayer or action	emotion or intellect

Jesus said, "I came into the world for this: to bear witness to the truth; and all who are on the side of truth listen to my voice." "Truth?" said Pilate. "What is that?" (Jn 18:37–38).

Pilate is a man who has grown up enjoying all the cultural and intellectual benefits of the Roman Empire. But when it comes to recognizing the truth, Pilate is at a loss. "Truth? What is that?" There are so many philosophies, so many religions. Who is to say what the truth is?

What does it mean to say that Jesus is the truth? What kind of truth does he reveal?

According to Catholic faith, Jesus is the truth of human existence. To know Jesus is to begin to understand what it means to be human. Jesus is the measure and model of every person's life. To say that Jesus is our model does not mean that we must dress like a first century Galilean and speak Hebrew. It means that we must live the way that he lived. We must live in his Spirit. To live the truth that Jesus offers means that we must respond to the challenges of our life and society in the same spirit that he did.

Not only does Jesus reveal the truth of what it means to be a human being, but he also reveals the truth of God's love for us. Jesus is also the answer to the question. "What is God like?" For it is the belief of Christians that Jesus is unique in all of human history. As deeply as any human beings may follow Christ, they can never become his equal. Jesus is not another of the great teachers in history. In Jesus we come face to face with God.

For Personal Reflection

Some people believe that it is unimportant what you believe as long as you believe in something. Do you agree with this?

At another point in John's Gospel Jesus says, "The truth will set you free." Do you think that the truth that we discover in science and the arts can also bring us closer to God?

Several young couples gather together at an ocean beach house. They share some food, fun and beer, and one of them says, "Ah, this is the life." You have probably seen a hundred variations of this commercial on television trying to sell you anything from beer to toilet paper. The advertising that we are bombarded with sells us more than a product, it sells us an entire way of life with promises of happiness.

Jesus saw himself as "the Life." In fact, he identified his mission with it: "I have come that they may have life and have it to the full" (Jn 10:10). However, the life that Jesus offers is different from the natural happiness of good food and friends, although it certainly does not exclude them. The life that Jesus offers is what Christians have traditionally called "grace." Grace is the presence and work of God in our lives. The effect of God's grace is to change us—to make us more like him. In John's Gospel, Jesus refers to this type of life as eternal life. Most of us probably think of eternal life as life that goes on forever, but this is not its primary meaning. Eternal life is a quality of life. It is the fulfillment of our relationship with God, and it begins in this life and not only when we die. It is also one of the few things that Jesus ever defines:

> And eternal life is this:
> to know you the only true God,
> and Jesus Christ whom you sent (Jn 17:3).

The life that Jesus offers is the "good life" not because it satisfies all our basic needs and supplies us with our creaturely comforts, but because it offers us a joy that fills our deepest longings for happiness: "I have told you all this that my joy may be in you and your joy may be complete" (Jn 15:11).

For Personal Reflection

1. What do you think constitutes the "good life"?

2. What do you think is the difference between happiness and joy? Do you know anyone that you would call a joyful person? What do you think makes such a person that way?

Jesus, the Lamb of God

> The next day, seeing Jesus coming toward him, John said, "Look, there is the lamb of God that takes away the sin of the world" (Jn 1:29).

These are familiar words to Catholics. They have become part of the liturgy of the Eucharist. But where does this expression "lamb of God" come from? In fact there are a number of interpretations that the scholars point to, but we will focus on one: the Passover lamb.

Every year the Jewish people celebrate the Passover to recall the great saving event of God in freeing them from slavery in Egypt. As you may recall the Jews smeared the blood of the lamb over the doorposts and the angel of death "passed over." Thus, they were "saved" by the blood of the lamb. Each year at the seder meal of the Passover feast, they were to relive the experience of the exodus when God freed them from bondage. They were to slaughter the Passover lamb as a reminder of God's saving act.

John uses this feast of the Jews to explain who Jesus is. He is the new lamb. It is now his blood that brings salvation. In John's Gospel, Jesus is killed on the day before the Passover. This is the day that the lambs are slaughtered in preparation for the feast. John is comparing Jesus to the lamb. Like the lamb, none of Jesus' bones are broken. By calling Jesus the lamb of God John is teaching that Jesus is now the sacrifice that brings salvation.

For Personal Reflection

The "lamb of God" image emphasizes the sacrifice that Jesus made. Do you think sacrifice is an essential element of loving? When is sacrifice a part of your lifestyle?

Jesus, the Bread of Life

Most of us get a little embarrassed when our stomach growls in public. It is usually a sign of the fact that we are hungry. However, food is not the only human hunger. Some people hunger for money, others for power or prestige. There are also those who hunger for God. In the Old Testament the psalmist wrote about it this way: "As a doe longs for running streams, so my soul yearns for you my God" (Ps 42:1). How can our hunger for God find nourishment?

> I am the bread of life.
> He who comes to me will never be hungry;
> he who believes in me will never thirst (Jn 6:35).

When John refers to Jesus as the bread of life, he is appealing to a Christian custom and ritual that is now already sixty years old. When John mentions the bread of life, his readers will immediately think of the Eucharist. From its earliest days, members of the Church met for what was originally called "the breaking of the bread." John wants to emphasize its importance and centrality to Christian faith. Oddly, however, he is the only one of the evangelists who does not include the story of the Last Supper. Instead, John uses Chapter 6 of his Gospel to teach about the Eucharist. His main point is that Christians still have access to Jesus through the Eucharist, the bread of life: "He who eats my flesh and drinks my blood lives in me and I live in him" (Jn 6:56).

For Personal Reflection

The great spiritual leader of India, Mahatma Gandhi, once said, "For those who are hungry, God may often take the appearance of bread." He was not talking about the Eucharist. What do you think he meant? What do you think is meant by a hunger for God?

The Followers of Jesus

The writings in the New Testament that we attribute to John (the Gospel and three letters) are not only interested in describing

Jesus; they are also interested in explaining the responsibilities of those who follow Christ. Perhaps nowhere in the Gospels do we find such an insight into the relationship between faith and love. For John, these two virtues are inseparable. This point is brought out in his Gospel in the story of the Last Supper. For the Christians of the early Church (as well as today) the Eucharist is at the heart of their faith. It is at the Eucharist that the risen Lord is present. However, John wants to make it clear that the Eucharist is more than a ritual; it is an entire way of life. He does not include the story of the meal itself, but instead tells how Jesus washed the feet of his apostles:

> Jesus knew that the Father had put everything into his hands, and that he had come from God and was returning to God, and he got up from the table, removed his outer garment and, taking a towel, wrapped it around his waist; he then poured water into a basin and began to wash the disciples' feet and to wipe them with the towel he was wearing. . . .
>
> When he had washed their feet and put on his clothes again he went back to the table. "Do you understand," he said, "what I have done to you? You call me Master and Lord, and rightly; so I am. If I, then, the Lord and Master, have washed your feet, you should wash each other's feet. I have given you an example so that you may copy what I have done to you" (Jn 13:3–5; 12–15).

This is the story that John tells instead of the breaking of the bread and the sharing of the cup. It is a story of love and service, and John means to associate it with the Eucharist. The Eucharist is not meant to be only something that we do in church. It involves an entire way of life, a life of love and service. It seems that John is saying that unless we *live* the Eucharist, the ritual itself will become empty. John spells out this connection between faith and love in Chapter 15:

As the Father has loved me
so have I loved you.
Remain in my love.
If you keep my commandments
you will remain in my love,
just as I have kept the Father's commandments
and remain in his love.
I have told you this
so that my joy may be in you
and your joy may be complete.
This is my commandment:
love one another as I have loved you (Jn 15:9–12).

For Personal Reflection

Loving others seems to depend somewhat on loving ourselves first. What's the difference between a healthy love of self and being conceited or self-centered? What is necessary for a healthy love of self?

Concluding Remarks

Before we conclude our look at this Gospel, it may help to answer two more questions: first, who wrote this Gospel? Second, why is it so different from the others?

We are not really sure who the author of John's Gospel is. Tradition has associated it with John the apostle. However, biblical scholars tell us that it wasn't his hand that composed it. It was probably written by one of John's disciples after his death and then edited by others. It may have been John's teaching and preaching that inspired it, but the actual writing was done by others.

Why is it so different? John's Gospel seems to interpret the teaching and person of Jesus into a different and exciting way of explaining who Jesus was. He tells the story of Jesus but puts it much more into his own words. The Gospel is a teaching device, and John (or the author), like any good teacher, explains the truth in a way that can be best understood by his audience. The result is an accurate but different rendering of the person of Jesus.

Questions for Review

1. What are five key differences between the Gospel of John and the Synoptic Gospels?

2. What is the main theme of the Prologue to John's Gospel? What is the climax of the Prologue?

3. Why does John refer to Jesus as the Word?

4. How does John use the symbols of light and darkness?

5. What does the Gospel mean when it says that Jesus is the truth?

6. Why is Jesus called the "lamb of God"?

7. How is John's account of the Last Supper different from that of the Synoptics? Where does he teach about the Eucharist?

8

Portraits of the Early Church

Until now, we have concentrated our efforts on the Gospels and the person and teaching of Jesus. In this chapter we will see how the remaining books of the New Testament give us important insight into the development of Christian faith and the ongoing understanding of our relationship to God. These books include one book of religious history (the Acts of the Apostles), twenty-one letters written by various leaders of the Church, and one book of apocalyptic literature (the Book of Revelation). It is not our purpose to study these in depth. Rather, we will examine some of the major themes and characters in them as a group.

The Unleashing of the Spirit

Fear—we have all experienced it at one point or another. Maybe it was the local bully, or the domineering teacher, or the look in your father's eye after you had pushed him too far. For the followers of Jesus, it was the thought of ending up the same way that he did. The Acts of the Apostles tells us that the apostles were terrified after Jesus' death. And yet something changed all that. They went from a frightened group to bold proclaimers of faith in Jesus, men who would put their life on the line for the faith. What changed all this? The Spirit who had been at the heart of Jesus was now in their own hearts. Luke describes it this way:

> When Pentecost day had come around, they had all met in one room, when suddenly they heard what sounded to be a powerful wind from heaven, the noise of which filled the entire house in which they were sitting; and something appeared to them that seemed like tongues of fire; these separated and came to rest on the head of each of them. They were all filled with the Holy Spirit and began to speak foreign languages as the Spirit gave them the gift of speech (Acts 2:1–4).

What had happened? The apostles were filled with the Holy Spirit. They were changed men. Jesus' death marked a new beginning: the age of the Spirit. It seems that the followers of Jesus were now capable of wisdom and action that they had not been capable of before Jesus' death. In fact, in John's Gospel Jesus says, "Still, I must tell you the truth; it is for your own good that I am going because unless I go the Advocate (the Holy Spirit) will not come to you; but if I do go I will send him to you" (Jn 16:7). Jesus seems to be saying that the Holy Spirit has a role that he (Jesus) cannot fulfill while on earth.

What does this story tell us about the Holy Spirit? The Spirit is associated with wind throughout the Bible, and Luke also uses the image here. Just as the wind hovered over the abyss at the dawn of creation, now the wind signifies a new creation. The grace and love of God has now been revealed in a powerful new way. Human beings have reached a new depth in their relationship with God. The Father not only has sent his Son to live among us, he has sent their Spirit to live within us.

The first effect of the Spirit is to free the apostles from their fear. Filled with the Spirit, the disciples go out to proclaim the good news. It is their fear that has held them back, and now their fear has been replaced with the life of God.

The next effect on the apostles is a peculiar one. They begin to speak in foreign tongues. This is a charism or gift of the Holy Spirit known as glossalalia or the gift of tongues. This charismatic gift seemed to be fairly widespread in the early Church, and it is not uncommon today among charismatic prayer groups. These are Christians who emphasize the role and presence of the Holy Spirit. In the story of Pentecost, we see that the purpose of the gift is to bring unity to different peoples: "They were amazed and astonished. 'Surely,' they said, 'all these men speaking are Galileans? How does it happen that each of us hears them in our own native language?' " (Acts 2:7–8). Thus the Spirit unites what was divided. This story seems to parallel the story of the tower of Babel in the Book of Genesis (Gen 11). In that story the presence of many languages is the result of sin, and it brings with it confusion. The Spirit is the opposite. Through the gift of tongues people are united. This is one of the most important aspects of the Spirit. Wherever it is present, people are joined together in love and understanding.

The final effect of the Spirit in this story is the very creation of the Church. Because of the Spirit the disciples become witnesses for the faith. The followers of Jesus now have a mission and role in God's plan of salvation. Peter assumes the role of leadership and begins to preach their new faith:

Men of Israel, listen to what I am going to say: Jesus the Nazarene was a man commended to you by God by the miracles and portents and signs that God worked through him when he was among you, as you all know. This man, who was put into your power by the deliberate intention and foreknowledge of God, you took and had crucified by men outside the law. You killed him, but God raised him to life. . . . For this reason the whole house of Israel can be certain that God has made this Jesus whom you crucified both Lord and Christ (Acts 2:22–24, 36).

This summarizes the faith of the Church. Jesus is recognized finally for who he really is. The followers of Jesus no longer see him simply as Teacher and Master; he is Lord and Christ. The Spirit leads us to Jesus the Lord.

For Personal Reflection

The Spirit enters our life in a special way in the sacrament of confirmation. Is this sacrament simply a memory or a reality that you try to live? St. Paul lists the fruits of the Spirit as love, joy, patient endurance, kindness, generosity, faith, mildness and chastity. Which of these is most present in your life? Which is most in need of cultivation?

Paul

We mentioned earlier that Jesus was remarkable in the way that he turned people's lives around. Fishermen became leaders of the Church, prostitutes became saints, tax collectors and sinners became loyal believers. Even after his death and resurrection, when people encountered Christ, their life would never again be the same. A case in point is Paul or Saul of Tarsus. Paul was the greatest thinker and missionary of the early Church and wrote many of the letters in the New Testament (fourteen are attributed to him). Yet when he was a young man he seemed an unlikely candidate for such prominence in the Church.

Paul was a very devout Jew who was a member of the Pharisee party and studied under the great rabbi Gamaliel. It is possible that Paul himself was a rabbi. Paul looked on Christianity as an extremely dangerous heretical sect which was following a false prophet. If allowed to flourish, he feared that this new group could do great damage to Judaism and the law of Moses. Paul actively persecuted the Church and was present at the death of its first martyr, Stephen (Acts 7:54–8:3). He was on his way to Damascus to arrest the followers of Jesus when an extraordinary event occurred that changed his life forever:

> Suddenly, while he was traveling to Damascus and just before he reached the city, there came a light from heaven all around him. He fell to the ground and then he heard a voice saying, "Saul, Saul, why are you persecuting me?" "Who are you, Lord?" he asked and the voice answered, "I am Jesus, and you are persecuting me. Get up now and go into the city and you will be told what you have to do" (Acts 9:3–6).

Paul went back to Damascus where he was baptized and instructed in the faith. He later went to Jerusalem where he met Peter. Before long, it was decided that he should make a missionary journey to bring the Gospel to the cities of Asia Minor. Eventually, he made three such journeys. Wherever he went, he first proclaimed the Gospel to the Jews in their synagogues. However, he encountered little success with his Jewish brothers, and when rejected by them, he preached to the Gentiles (non-Jews). His great success with the pagans earned him the title "Apostle to the Gentiles." Paul founded many Christian communities on these journeys, and his letters to these communities give us the clearest picture of life in the early Church.

For Personal Reflection

Paul is certainly not the only great Christian to undergo a profound change or conversion in his life. St. Augustine, St. Francis, St. Thomas à Becket, Thomas Merton and Dorothy Day were also great examples of conversion. Read about their lives in the New Catholic Encyclopedia.

The End of the World

The early Church believed that Jesus would return soon to finally establish God's kingdom and fulfill his plan of salvation. The second coming of the Lord, or the parousia, as it was called, had a great impact on the way that the Church understood itself and its mission. They lived in expectation of the end of the world and the Lord's return, and they even prayed for it. Paul's first letter deals with this concern. Apparently the Christian community in Thessalonica had become very worried about the fate of Christians who had died before the Lord's return. Would they be saved or would salvation be only for those who were present at the Lord's second coming? Paul writes to reassure them that the living will have no advantage over the dead:

> We want you to be quite certain brothers, about those who have died, to make sure that you do not grieve about them, like the other people who have no hope. We believe that Jesus died and rose again, and that it will be the same for those who died in Jesus: God will bring them with him. We can tell you this from the Lord's own teaching, that any of us who are left alive until the Lord's coming will have no advantage over those who have died (1 Thes 4:13–15).

But when will Jesus return? Paul does not know, but like the rest of the Church, he seemed to believe that it would not be long. In fact, he includes himself in the group who will be present at the second coming. In fact, of course, Paul was wrong. Two thousand years later we continue to wonder when the end of the world will come. Enemies of the early Church tried to use the delayed return of the Lord to attack the faith. Because the parousia had not occurred as believed, they claimed that the entire Christian message was false. The Second Letter of Peter denounces these people and says that the delay is a manifestation of God's divine patience:

We must be careful to remember that during the last days there are bound to be people who are scornful, the kind who always please themselves in what they do, and they will make fun of the promise and ask, "Well, when is this coming? Everything goes on as it has since the fathers died, as it has since it began at the creation. . . . The Lord is not being slow to carry out his promises as anyone else might be called slow; but he is being patient with you all, wanting nobody to be lost and everybody to be brought to change his ways. . . . What we are waiting for is what he promised: a new heaven and a new earth, the place where righteousness will be at home (2 Pet 3:3–4, 9, 13).

The Christians of the early Church were forced to rethink their ideas about the end of the world and the day of salvation. Their faith did not give them a crystal ball into the future. God would act in his own way. There are some groups today who believe that the parousia is about to occur. They base their beliefs on things that are said in the New Testament, often in the Book of Revelation. They believe that this book contains secret symbols that show that the end is near. Unfortunately, Christians have been saying the same thing for nearly two thousand years. Each generation has those people who are convinced that the Book of Revelation is talking about them. Each generation has been wrong. In fact, the New Testament, including the Book of Revelation, is writing about its own age. The Book of Revelation was written at a time when the Church was suffering great persecution from Rome. Its message was one of hope—that in the midst of terrible persecution, Christians must endure, confident of God's justice and vindication.

Does the New Testament tell us when the end of the world will occur? It clearly does not. Those who interpret the New Testament in such a way are merely repeating the mistakes made throughout the history of the Church.

For Personal Reflection

What do you imagine is the future of planet earth?

The Church

What do you think of when you hear the word "Church"? A building? Sunday mornings? The pastor of your parish? Many people identify the Church with a building or with the priests and nuns who work in the parish. When we read the New Testament, however, we come away with a much different notion of Church.

The early Church saw itself primarily as a community of faith. They were those who had been baptized into Christ and had received his Spirit. In many cases it meant a dramatic new way of living, a call to live in holiness and to abandon the ways of sin that the world lived in. Today it is difficult for many of us to identify with this understanding. For better or worse, we grew up in the Church. We were baptized as infants and never knew anything other than the religion we were taught. For many people today the Church does not represent anything dramatic at all. Belonging to it requires no great inner change of heart, no new way of life. It may be hard for us to relate to Paul's words to the Church at Ephesus:

> And you were dead, through the crimes and sins in which you used to live when you were following the way of this world, obeying the ruler who governs the air, the spirit who is at work in the rebellious. . . . But God loved us so much that he was generous with his mercy; when we were dead through our sins, he brought us to life with Christ (Eph 2:1, 4–5).

The Church was to be a community of those who had given up their former lives and taken on the life of holiness. In this way, the Church was to be God's vehicle in the world. God would be present in the Church in a special way. The Church, not as a building but as a people, was to be a dwelling place for God:

> You are a part of a building that has the apostles and prophets for its foundations, and Christ Jesus himself for the main cornerstone. As every structure is aligned on him, all grow into one holy temple in the Lord; and you too, in him, are being built into a house where God lives, in the Spirit (Eph 2:20–22).

In this passage Paul uses the image of a building to describe the Church. It is, however, only an analogy. Christ is the cornerstone, the apostles are the foundation and the people are the building. This is Church that is built on flesh and blood. It is a living thing.

The most famous image that Paul uses to describe the Church is found in the First Letter to the Corinthians. Here Paul describes the Church as the body of Christ. He compares the Church to a human body in which all the different parts have different functions and yet all are essential and important. Paul's understanding of the Church emphasizes the diversity within the Church and sees that as something good and necessary. People will come in all different shapes, sizes, colors, and ages, and they will have different talents and personalities, but it is all for the good of the community. The heart and soul of this community is the Holy Spirit who is the creative and unifying power within it.

> There is a variety of gifts but always the same Spirit; there are all sorts of service to be done, but always to the same Lord; working in all sorts of different ways in different people, it is the same God who is working in all of them. . . .
>
> Just as a human body, though it is made up of many parts, is a single unit because all of these parts, though many, make one body, so it is with Christ. In the one Spirit we were

all baptized, Jews as well as Greeks, slaves as well as citizens, and one Spirit was given us all to drink.

Nor is the body to be identified with any one of its parts. If the foot were to say, "I am not a hand and so I do not belong to the body," would that mean that it stopped being part of the body? If your whole body was just one eye, how would you hear anything? If it was just one ear, how would you smell anything?

Instead of that, God put all the separate parts into the body on purpose. If all the parts were the same how could it be a body? As it is the parts are many, but the body is one. . . .

Now you together are Christ's body (1 Cor 12:4–6, 12–20, 27).

There are two key points that Paul is making here. The first, as we have already seen, is that diversity is important and necessary within the Christian community. The second is that the Church is now to be the presence of Christ in the world. Jesus continues to live, and he lives primarily in the community of faith, the Church. We are to be his intelligence, goodness, forgiveness, healing, compassion and service to the world. For Paul, the Church is a body that makes Christ present in the world and is animated by his Spirit.

Even though Paul had this beautiful image of the Church, he realized that he was describing an ideal. In fact, the Church was not only filled with saints but with sinners still deeply in need of change. In the very same letter, Paul criticizes his fellow Christians for immoral sexual behavior, bickering and divisions, and even for getting drunk at the Eucharist. No one knew the human limitations of the Church better than Paul, and yet Paul saw that it was precisely in this imperfect community that the Spirit of God was also at work.

For Personal Reflection

1. What are some examples of the Church as the body of Christ in today's world? How do the different gifts and talents serve the whole body? Where do you fit into the body?

2. In what ways is the Church human and in what ways divine?

The Council of Jerusalem

The Church was not very old when it faced its first major crisis. The problem centered around the relationship between Christian faith and Judaism. At first the entire Church was Jewish. Jesus was a Jew and he had confined his mission to the people of Israel. The apostles and the followers of Jesus continued to think of themselves as Jews. Jesus had not traveled to the great pagan cities to convert the people, nor had he negated the truths of the faith of Israel. There was no good reason for the apostles to stop the practice of their Jewish faith, and there was no reason to believe that the Gospel should be preached to the Gentiles.

Before long, however, this began to become a problem. Paul and others had taken the message of the Gospel to the Gentiles and had converted many of them to faith in Christ. These people knew nothing of the Jewish law and customs, but they had come to accept Jesus as Lord. Would these Gentile converts be forced to obey the Jewish law as well as becoming followers of Jesus through baptism? In particular, would the men have to be circumcised, the physical sign of belonging to the faith of Israel? The Gentiles knew nothing of the religious tradition of circumcision, and Paul feared that it might frighten some of them away.

Paul was very clear in his thinking on this issue. Christians were saved not by the law of Moses but through faith in Christ. The law was all well and good, but it was not essential for salvation. (In a letter written to the people in the Church at Rome, Paul spells out his thinking on this issue at length.) There were many in the Church who could not accept Paul's new progressive ideas. These people, known as Judaizers, condemned Paul for being unfaithful to the Mosaic law and the traditions of Israel. They insisted that Gentile converts be circumcised and obey the law of Moses. Finally a meeting was called in Jerusalem that brought together the major leaders of the Church to discuss the issue.

Peter, who had personally baptized a Roman officer, defended Paul and his thinking:

> "My brothers," he said, "you know perfectly well in the early days God made his choice among you: the pagans were to learn the good news from me and so become believers. In fact God, who can read everyone's heart, showed his approval of them by giving the Holy Spirit to them just as he had to us. God made no distinction between them and us, since he purified their hearts through faith. It would only provoke God's anger now, surely, if you imposed on the disciples the very burden that neither we nor our ancestors were strong enough to support. Remember, we believe that we are saved the same way that they are: through the grace of the Lord Jesus (Acts 15:7b–11).

Peter was followed by James who was the leader of the conservative Jewish community. James proposed a compromise that allowed the Gentiles to go uncircumcised but sought that they follow some of the Jewish dietary laws. Even with the compromise, the council of Jerusalem was saying that the Mosaic law was unnecessary for salvation.

So what's all the fuss about? Why is this council so important? The effect of the council on the future of the Church can hardly be measured. Instead of being tied to the Jewish community by the law of Moses, the Church was now free to bring the good news to all peoples and cultures. It was free to use the different cultural customs to help express the meaning of the faith. It was on its way to becoming catholic in the truest sense of the word: universally open and all-embracing.

For Personal Reflection

1. The Catholic faith today embraces countless cultures around the world. In each culture the faith is the same and yet its expression will reflect the people of that country. Can you think of some examples of how the faith reflects the people of various cultures?

2. Another dramatic council of the Church occurred much more recently. From 1962–1965, bishops throughout the world met in Rome for the Second Vatican Council. The council has had an extraordinary effect on the Church. Ask some oldtimers like your parents or grandparents to describe some of the changes in the Church that they have experienced.

Questions for Review

1. What were some of the effects of Pentecost on the apostles?

2. Describe Paul's background and conversion to Christ.

3. What did the believers of the early Church believe about the second coming of Jesus? Does the New Testament tell us when this will occur?

4. Explain Paul's description of the Church as the body of Christ.

5. What was debated at the council of Jerusalem? Why was this council so important to the future of the Church?

9

A Summary of the Books of the New Testament

A book of this nature and size is not meant to cover everything in the Bible. What we have tried to do is capture the most important themes and ideas that run through the Bible and how they came to be formed. In this chapter we will briefy summarize the main ideas in each of the books of the New Testament. Since we have treated the Gospels at some length, we will not review them here. In order to put some continuity to these works we will treat them in approximate chronological order. (It is only approximate because the dates of these works are not always known with certitude.)

The First Epistle of Paul to the Thessalonians (ca. 51)

This epistle or letter is the earliest written document in the New Testament and for that reason alone it is important. What problems and concerns do we find in the early days of the Church? The big one in this letter is the question of Jesus's return. The people of Thessalonica are upset because there are some who have died awaiting the return of the Lord. What will happen to them? Paul tells them not to worry and assures them that the living will have no advantage over the dead at the Lord's return. This letter reinforces what we have already seen—the early Church expected the second coming within their lifetime.

The Second Epistle of Paul to the Thessalonians (ca. 52)

If at first you don't succeed, try, try again. That's probably how Paul felt writing this letter to Thessalonica. Many Christians there still believed that the Lord's return was imminent. Unfortunately they seemed to take on the attitude that the next world was the important one and that responsibilities to this life could be ignored. Paul sets them straight and emphasizes that the life of the Christian must be lived here and now.

The Epistle of Paul to the Galatians (ca. 55)

The problems in Thessalonica were simple compared to the ones that Paul later faced, and we see reflected in this letter to the churches of Galatia. The problem is one that we have already mentioned—the relationship between Christian faith and the Jewish law. Paul had been personally attacked by Judaizers as not being one of the original apostles and therefore lacking authority. These people preached a different version of the Gospel to the people of Galatia, one that included adherence to the Mosaic law. Paul writes an emotional and angry letter. "Are you people in Galatia mad?" he writes. He emphasizes his great theme: faith in Christ is the way to salvation.

The letters to the Thessalonians and the Galatians reveal that Paul had a dual role in the early Church: he was both a practical pastor and a great theologian. The problems that he confronts in these letters are not simply theoretical ones. They have very important consequences in the life of the people.

For Personal Reflection

What do you think are some of the important issues facing the Church in your diocese? What are the most important issues

that the Church should be confronting in America and in the
world? Do you think that there are any modern day "Pauls" who
are speaking out? Who are they?

The First Epistle of Paul to the Corinthians (ca. 56)

There is sometimes the impression that life in the early Christian communities was very ideal and that over the course of the
centuries the Church has corrupted the original beauty of their lifestyle. In fact, it is not that simple. The Church has always been a
combination of sinner and saint and those in between. The early
Church had more than its share of heroes, but it also had some
problems that make ours today seem pale. The community in Corinth seems to be the best example of this. Corinth was a seaport
city that attracted many travelers and different types of people.
Like some seaports today, it was famous for its wild lifestyle. Sexual immorality was rampant, and the phrase "Corinthian woman"
was slang for a prostitute. Yet Paul enjoyed a good deal of success
in his visit and stay in the city. He lived there for about a year and
a half and established a strong community of faith. He wrote this
letter about four years after he had left Corinth, and much had
happened within the community since he had gone.

The city had been visited by a great Christian preacher named
Apollos. Unfortunately, the result was division within the community. Some were saying that they sided with Apollos, others
were with Paul, still others with Peter. Paul tries to make clear to
them that the heart of the faith is the person of Jesus and not the
preacher who teaches them. In line with this, he later goes on to
explain the Church as the body of Christ, as we have already seen
in an earlier chapter.

The letter continues to treat many practical and doctrinal
problems within the community. It seems that some of the Corinthians were returning to their old habits of sexual immorality. Paul
tries to explain to them that the body is also part of the spiritual
person. In fact, their bodies are to be treated with respect because

they are now "temples of the Holy Spirit." Another problem that Paul had to deal with was behavior at the Mass, or "the breaking of the bread" as it was known then. In those days the Eucharist was held in the homes of the people and was accompanied by a meal. It turns out that some people were getting drunk while others were not getting anything to eat. This was hardly the "ideal Church."

This letter is important because it gives us such a clear picture into the life of one of the early Christian communities. However, Paul also takes on some important theological issues in this letter as well, including the resurrection, the Church, the role of the Holy Spirit and marriage. What we find in this letter is a picture of the Church being guided by the Spirit and yet struggling to shed its old ideas and way of life.

The Second Epistle of Paul to the Corinthians (ca. 57)

We are not really sure of the effects of Paul's first letter to Corinth because the problems that he addressed are not mentioned in the second epistle. Here Paul has once again taken up the task of describing the trials of his ministry and defending his authority as an apostle.

For Personal Reflection

Corinth is a church "guided by the Spirit and yet struggling to shed its old ideas and way of life." Do you think that statement could be said for the Church today? What are some of the old ideas and habits that we need to change to become better Christians?

The Epistle of Paul to the Philippians (ca. 53 or 58 or 62)

Why three different dates for this letter? We know that it was written while Paul was imprisoned; however, we do not know which imprisonment. Some say Ephesus (53), others Caesarea

(58), and still others Rome (62). The place and date are not as important as the theme. In prison Paul is experiencing deeply the role of humility and suffering service, and the letter reflects this experience. He uses Jesus as his model and as the model for all Christians in their life of humility. Paul sees the human nature of Jesus as the ultimate expression of humility:

> There must be no competition among you, no conceit; but everybody is to be self-effacing. Always consider the other person to be better than yourself, so that nobody thinks of his own interests first but everybody thinks of other people's interest instead. In your minds you must be the same as Christ Jesus:
>
>> His state was divine,
>> yet he did not cling to his equality with God
>> but emptied himself
>> to assume the condition of a slave,
>> and became as men are;
>> and being as all men are,
>> he was humbler yet,
>> even to accepting death,
>> death on a cross.
>> But God raised him high
>> and gave him the name
>> which is above all other names
>> so that all beings
>> in the heavens, on earth and in the underworld,
>> should bend the knee at the name of Jesus
>> and that every tongue should acclaim
>> Jesus Christ as Lord,
>> to the glory of God the Father (Phil 2:3–11).

The Epistle of Paul to the Romans (ca. 59)

So far we have seen that Paul's epistles are often very inspired by the real life problems of the community. The Letter to the Romans is something of an exception to that rule. In this epistle, more than any others, Paul's main concern seems to be theological; that is, he is interested in developing the ideas concerning salvation by faith and the role of the Mosaic law. For this reason, Romans can be a very difficult letter although it ranks among the most important that Paul wrote. Once again, Paul restates his belief that it is through the grace of God that we have been saved and not through obedience to the law. We cannot accomplish our own salvation by an act of will power. Paul sees the human race as being torn in two directions—good and evil—and as such is dependent on God's grace. It is God's free gift of love for us that brings salvation. We cannot and need not earn it.

For Personal Reflection

Paul seems to be saying that salvation is a gift from God, yet at other times he stresses the need of the Christian to live a life of love and humility (as in Philippians). How do you think these ideas are related to each other?

The Epistle of Paul to the Ephesians (ca. 61–63)

If I wanted this book to sell more copies and have greater impact, I could put the name of some great Scripture scholar on the cover. It wouldn't be very honest, and I would probably be involved in a lawsuit. However, this was not an uncommon practice back in the days of St. Paul. In fact a number of letters attributed to Paul were not really written by him. They might have been written by those who knew him, and that fact gave greater weight to their ideas. Ephesians is probably one of those letters. The letter is important for its description of the universal and cosmic role of Christ in God's plan of salvation:

> He has let us know the mystery of his purpose, the hidden
> plan he so kindly made in Christ from the beginning to act

upon when the time had run their course to the end: that he would bring everything together under Christ, as head, everything in the heavens and everything on earth (Eph 1:9–10).

In this passage, there is a different interpretation of the person of Christ. He is the purpose of all creation, the one in whom all things find their meaning.

The Epistle of Paul to the Colossians (ca. 61–63)
This is another of Paul's letters written while in prison. We find in it another hymn concerning the universal role of Christ, as this understanding of Jesus begins to become more prominent in the life of the Church:

> He is the image of the unseen God
> and the first born of all creation,
> for in him were created
> all things in heaven and on earth. . . .
> Before anything was created, he existed,
> and he holds all things in unity (Col 1:15–17).

For Personal Reflection

The understanding of the cosmic Christ that is presented in these two epistles fits in well with an evolutionary understanding of the world. If the world is in a state of evolution, perhaps there is a "spiritual" evolution going on as well—that the Spirit is slowly but inexorably leading mankind toward God. What do you think?

The Epistle of Paul to Philemon (ca. 61–63)
One of the topics that we discussed at the beginning of this book was the meaning of the Bible as the inspired Word of God.

We noted that the Scriptures reflect the guiding presence of the Holy Spirit, but that they also reflect the historical and cultural beliefs of the people who wrote them. Paul's letter to Philemon is a good example of this. It is more like a personal letter than an epistle to a community. It concerns itself with Onesimus, Philemon's runaway slave who has since converted to Christianity. Paul has converted Onesimus and has sent him back to his master. Paul implores forgiveness from Philemon, reminding him that he and his slave are brothers in Christ. At the time it was written, slavery was an accepted fact of life, and Paul's outlook seems to reflect this belief. Paul does nothing to change Philemon's outlook on slavery. He is limited by his own cultural background. However, Paul does see a new relationship for them. Onesimus is not only a slave but a brother in Christ.

For Personal Reflection

Some people distort the Word of God by claiming that every statement in it reflects the will of God. For example, they could use the letter to Philemon to justify slavery. Can you think of any other examples?

The Epistle of James (ca. 62)

This is the first epistle that we have seen in this chapter that is not attributed to Paul. Who is James? He was the leader of the community of Christians, living in Jerusalem, known for its Jewish personality. The letter itself reads like a New Testament version of the Book of Proverbs, full of advice and wise sayings on a wide variety of topics.

The First Epistle of Peter (ca. 65)

Most scholars doubt that Peter wrote this letter in his own hand. It may, however, be the work of one close to Peter at the time of his death. It is actually more like a sermon than an epistle, describing the spiritual and moral qualities of the Christian life.

The Epistle to the Hebrews (ca. 70)

The author of the Epistle to the Hebrews is unknown. The letter is mostly a theological treatment of the old and new covenant and the relationship between ritual sacrifice and the sacrifice of Jesus. This letter was written to Jewish Christians and makes clear that Jesus has replaced the old law, the old priesthood and the old sacrifices. The author of this letter also has a deep sense of the human nature of Jesus:

> For it is not as if we had a high priest who was incapable of feeling our weaknesses with us; but we have one who has been tempted in every way that we are, though he is without sin (Heb 4:15).

The First Epistle of Paul to Timothy (ca. 62–100)

So far in our discussion of the early Church we have mentioned apostles and disciples and prophets, but nothing about priests or bishops. When did they come to be a part of the Church? We first hear of them in this letter to Timothy and in a second letter to Timothy and one to Titus. These three are known as the "pastoral epistles" because they have so much to say about the structure of the early Church. As you can see from the dates listed above, there is a debate over who wrote these letters and when. Some scholars believe Paul to be the author, but most believe that the description of the Church in these letters is of one that existed only after Paul's death. It is in this letter that we see the churches being established on the authority of the bishop, the presbyter (priest) and the deacon, which is the structure still today.

The Second Epistle of Paul to Timothy (63–100)

This epistle also reflects one of the major concerns of the Church at the end of the first century—the importance of sound teaching and the danger of false teachers.

The Epistle of Paul to Titus (63–100)

This is the third of the "pastoral epistles" and shares the themes of the first two. Titus was Paul's companion on one of his missionary journeys and became an administrator of a church in Crete. This letter instructs him in the choice of leaders for the community. It is important for giving us a further look at the development of the Church in the first century.

For Personal Reflection

As the Church grew, it became more organized in its leadership and its teaching. Today, the Church is not only a community of faith but a vast institution as well. What are some of the reasons for having a vast and organized institution? Are there any drawbacks?

The Acts of the Apostles (ca. 85)

We finally come to a New Testament book that is not an epistle. The Acts of the Apostles is the story of the life of the early Church as conveyed by the author of the Gospel of Luke. Despite its title, the book focuses on the work of two of the Apostles, Peter and Paul. The story opens in Jerusalem shortly after Jesus' resurrection and concludes with the Gospel being preached in Rome, the great city of the Gentiles. In a real sense, the main character of this book is the Holy Spirit. For Luke, the journey from Jerusalem to Rome, with all its triumphs and hardships, is the mysterious work of the Spirit bringing the Gospel to the ends of the earth.

The Epistle of Jude (ca. 90)

A number of times throughout this book we have emphasized that the Christian is saved by faith, not obedience to the law. When some people hear this, they seem to think, "Great! Now I can do whatever I want!'' They misinterpret the Christian's approach to the law. It seemed that there were quite a few of these in the first century Church. They felt that they were freed from the law to live any life they wanted. In this letter, the author blasts these people who have taken up a life of sexual immorality. He uses the fire and brimstone approach—calling down God's punishment on them.

The First Epistle of John (ca. 90–100)

This is the first of three epistles from the author of the Fourth Gospel. This letter also warns against false teachers, but is better known for some of its beautiful passages on love. John emphasizes love as the heart and soul of the Christian life, that which unites us to God himself: ''God is love, and anyone who lives in love lives in God and God lives in him'' (Jn 4:16).

The Second Epistle of John (ca. 90–100)

The second letter deals with the same problem as the first: there are ''progressive'' false teachers who are corrupting the faith. Obedience to the law of love and faith in Christ are the only true ways to God.

The Third Epistle of John (ca. 90–100)

This is a very brief letter written to his friend Gaius condemning Diotrephes who refuses to accept the author or his envoys. We know little of the background to this letter, but once again it reveals a Church struggling to find unity.

For Personal Reflection

The Church in the first century had to do battle with ''false teachers.'' It became necessary to have a group who would officially declare what the Church believed or did not believe. This is the role of the magisterium, the teaching office of the Church, which consists of the Pope and bishops. Those things that are considered essential beliefs of the Church are called dogmas. What do you think are some of the dogmas of Catholic faith?

The Book of Revelation

The Book of Revelation is the most obscure and difficult to understand of all the books of the New Testament. The author of the book identifies himself as John, an exile on the island of Patmos. Traditionally, he has been identified as the author of the Fourth Gospel. Most scholars doubt that it is the same person, but many believe that it is reasonable to hold that the author is one of the disciples of John.

A quick glance at this work shows it to be filled with visions and symbols and language found nowhere else in the New Testament. In order to understand this work, it is important to understand the "literary form" or the type of literature that it represents. This is a literary form unique to the New Testament. It is not a Gospel, an epistle or religious history. It is an example of apocalyptic literature which uses symbolic images to portray the final struggle between good and evil. Written at a time when the Church was suffering persecution from the Roman Empire, it is addressed to seven churches, encouraging them to persevere and assuring them of God's final victory for them.

This book uses symbols and numbers to hide its true meaning. Rome is referred to as a beast with seven heads and ten horns (Rev 13:1). The seven heads refer to the hills upon which Rome is built, and the ten horns most likely refer to the ten-horned beast in the Book of Daniel which symbolized Epiphanes IV, one of the great persecutors of Israel. There is also in this book the infamous number 666: "If anyone is clever enough he may interpret the number of the beast: it is the number of a man, the number 666" (Rev 13:18). In the Hebrew and Greek alphabets, letters had a numerical value. If the name Caesar Nero were to be written in Hebrew, the number value of the Hebrew letters would add up to 666. It is not certain that this is the correct interpretation, but it makes a great deal of sense in the context of the book. Nero was the first of the Roman emperors to persecute the Church.

The Book of Revelation is a powerful piece of apocalyptic literature written at a time of great persecution. The battle between Rome and the Church is seen as part of the cosmic battle between God and Satan. Unfortunately, the Book of Revelation is often used today as an interpreter of present and future events. It has no such meaning. Its relevance today lies in its ability to point out the ongoing struggle between good and evil in the world and to encourage us not to lose heart in the face of such evil.

For Personal Reflection

In our culture, the Church does not have to live under the threat of persecution, but it continues to be a reality in many other parts of the world. Martyrs for the faith are as plentiful today as they have ever been. For an example, read of the life of Archbishop Romero of El Salvador.

The Second Epistle of Peter (ca. 100–140)

When this epistle was written, the resurrection of Jesus may have been a hundred years previous. Where was the second coming that the Church had always spoken of? There were those who used this fact to claim that the Church's teachings were all false. This letter is written to combat these people who are attacking the faith.

10

The Bible and Prayer

Recent surveys and polls taken in the United States indicate that many Americans pray on a regular basis. It would be interesting to discover what people do when they pray. What is it exactly that people consider to be prayer? In this chapter we will examine some of the dynamics of prayer and offer some practical suggestions on how to use the Bible for prayer.

What Is Prayer?

In order to understand prayer, let us begin by examining our earliest experiences of prayer and seeing what we can learn from them. Often children are taught to pray at an early age. Most often these prayers include asking God's blessing on special people and asking for his help in special situations. A child's typical prayer may say, "God bless mommy and daddy and Rover and please don't let it rain tomorrow because mommy is taking me to the zoo." One of the refreshing things about the prayer of children is that they will pray from the heart for the things that are really important to them. They will gladly pray for pets and leave out brothers and sisters with whom they may be fighting. The one thing that stands out about prayer is that *it is communication with God.*

Very often when we are children, we are taught certain prayers. These are prayers that are an important part of our faith and are passed down from one generation to the next. In the Christian tradition, the most famous prayer learned by children is the Lord's Prayer, also known as the Our Father. We are taught to memorize the prayer. Learning the prayer "by heart" can be the first step to living the prayer in the heart. However, there are also some dangers involved in this process. Too often we learn these prayers when we are too young to understand their meaning. We repeat the sounds and words, and when we do so we are told that we are praying. In fact, all that we are really doing is "parroting" the words. We repeat them without knowing what they mean. Let me offer a real life example. Many years ago, when my mother was putting the boys to bed and overhearing our prayers, she asked my older brother Peter to repeat the first sentence of the Our Father. "Our Father, who art in heaven, Howard be thy name," he said confidently. "Peter," she asked, "do you think God's first name is Howard?" Sure enough, he did. He had "parroted" the words hundreds of times, but since the real word "hallowed" meant nothing to him, he heard Howard and repeated it. It made sense, and I suppose that it must be nice to be on a first name basis with the Almighty.

This true story is one of thousands of examples (often funny) of parroting by children. The real problem occurs when this carries through adolescence and adulthood. It is important to remember that "saying prayers" is not necessarily praying. If these prayers help us to communicate with God, then indeed our prayers have become prayer.

Communication with God

So far we have described prayer as communication with God. Let us now look more closely at the meaning of this communication.

1. Communication is the life-blood of any relationship. Without communication, love and friendship are impossible. The deeper the level of the relationship, the deeper must the level of communication be between the two people. Strangers rarely become the recipients of our deepest feelings and thoughts. A true friend, however, is someone we let into our lives to share our joys and sorrows. We trust them. We know that we can reveal ourselves to them. If this is mutual, the friendship deepens and grows.

The same will hold true with our relationship with God. It will only be as good as the communication that takes place between him and ourselves. Thus prayer is the life-blood of faith. Without the communication of prayer, there is no real relationship.

2. God's communication is not limited to "religious" events like the sacraments or Mass. When we use the word "communication," people most often think of language and speech. However, educators and psychologists say that more than eighty percent of all communication is non-verbal. The way we look, the way we use our bodies, the way we act and the expression on our face are all forms of communication. God's means of communication are also diverse. God can communicate through nature, other people, events in our lives, our consciences, our feelings, and our intellect. All of life, then, is a possibility for prayer.

3. Communication is always a two-way street that involves listening as well as speaking. If you know people who are incapable of listening, you know what self-centered and boorish persons they are. People who only talk and never listen rarely have any relationships of depth in their lives. They never get to know anyone because they never listen.

Listening is one of the most important skills we will ever learn in our lifetime. It means to be open to the experience of life as lived by another. A good listener is someone who cares about us. It is someone who not only hears our words but hears *us*. When I was a student in college, I went through a period of time when I was very confused and depressed. I didn't really know what was bothering me, but I knew that I was unhappy. I went to talk with a priest who was recommended to me by a friend. I wound up seeing him every week for about six months. I couldn't believe how insightful he was. Then I realized that it was not so much what he said but the way that he listened that enabled me to open up and learn more about the things that were bothering me.

Prayer involves this same dynamic. We must be able to reveal ourselves freely and confidently with God. If we try to pretend to be the people that we think he wants us to be, the communication has ended. It is only when we are able to be open that we can in turn listen and discover the presence of God in the different aspects of our lives.

4. Communication is the source of union between two people. If you have an argument with someone, the only thing that will heal the argument is communication. If two people fall in love, the only thing that will enhance and develop that love is communication. In the deepest friendships, we see that the two people actually become parts of one another. The same is true with prayer. The more that we are able to communicate with God, the more our lives slowly reflect that communication. We develop a personal relationship with him. We begin to see and understand life differently. We begin to take on the attitudes and values of Jesus. This, of course, is a long lifetime process that we become involved in. It is a goal that we never reach completely, but it is the goal that gives shape to our lives.

Scripture and Prayer

One of the most important ways in which God communicates to us is through the Scriptures. In the Bible, we have the Word of God in a special way. The Bible is not simply another book in a collection of books. Through the Bible, God continues to reveal himself to us. For a Christian to develop a personal relationship with God, the Scriptures are essential. However, learning to pray with the Bible is a lot like learning to do anything else. It takes commitment and practice. In order to ease the process, I would suggest the following list of "don'ts."

1. DON'T open the Bible at random and expect to be inspired by God. While this may sometimes give results, it is a very poor technique for prayer.

2. DON'T interpret the Bible literally at all times. Try to apply some of the things that you have learned in this book. When Jesus says, "If your eye is a source of sin, pluck it out", he is engaging in typical Jewish exaggeration. Leave your eye alone, but get to the root of your sins and change.

3. DON'T always expect to "feel" inspired. There may be times when God feels close and other times when he seems a million miles away. This is normal in any prayer life. The important thing is that prayer be a commitment.

4. DON'T be too hard on yourself. Your prayer should reflect *your* life and relationship with God. You have not become a monk. Spend the amount of time that suits you best.

5. DON'T let your prayer become an escape from reality. Remember that you will not be judged by the number of hours

that you pray but by the quality of love in your life. Prayer should help you be a better person in your everyday life.

6. DON'T give up. If you should stop praying for a long time, maybe you needed the break. Remember that God is more interested in your return than in your absence.

Here are some suggestions of a more positive tone:

1. Plan your readings beforehand.

2. Find a quiet place where you know that you will be free of distractions for awhile.

3. Relax. Try to slow yourself down. One way to do this is to close your eyes and breathe slowly and deeply. Start with one deep breath. Over the next sixty seconds take half the number of breaths that you would normally take in a minute (the normal is usually around fifteen).

4. Read the passage that you have chosen.

5. Ask yourself: What is it that this passage is trying to teach me? How does it apply to my life now? (If the passage is from the Gospels, you might want to imagine yourself in the story as one of the characters and imagine your response.)

6. Finish with a closing prayer either in your own words or one that is special to you. Resolve to try to live the lesson of the reading *for that day*. Don't make grandiose promises to yourself. Take it one day at a time.

What Should I Read?

One of the biggest problems that people sometimes encounter is trying to decide what to read in the Bible. It's so big and confusing. Where do you start? The best practical suggestion here is to stay with the rest of the Church throughout the world. Everywhere throughout the world, the same readings are being read at Mass. If you are interested in praying with the Scriptures, it makes perfect sense to use the passages already chosen by the Church. These readings will take you through the great feasts and seasons of Advent and Christmas, Lent and Easter and Pentecost. A listing of these readings can be found in the missalette that is used in your parish.

Using a Prayer Journal

One of the most effective tools for prayer is the use of a journal. Writing can be very helpful to our prayer life. When we are forced to put our thoughts and feelings into words, we clarify them for ourselves. It also gives us a written memory. We can look back at our entries and see how we have changed and grown in our relationship with God. It can encourage us to continue on the journey.

Mini-Retreats

Finally, we suggest "mini-retreats" based on different passages from Scripture that focus on a certain theme. In order to help you with this, we have chosen a number of scriptural passages that reflect important aspects of our relationship with God. Seven passages are chosen for each theme, making the "mini-retreat" a week long. We are also listing one verse from the reading to focus on, but the entire selection should be read.

God's Love for You

1. Psalm 139:1–18	"It was you who created my inmost self, and put me together in my mother's womb."
2. Isaiah 49:15–16	"Does a woman forget her baby at the breast, or fail to cherish the son of her womb?"
3. Hosea 2:21–22	"I will betroth you to myself with faithfulness."
4. Luke 15:11–31	"His father saw him and was moved with pity. He ran to the boy, clasped him in his arms and kissed him tenderly."
5. Romans 8:35–39	"Nothing, therefore, can come between us and the love of Christ."
6. Ephesians 1:3–6	"Blessed be God the Father of our Lord Jesus Christ who has blessed us with all the spiritual blessings of heaven in Christ."
7. 1 John 3:1	"Think of the love that the Father has lavished on us."

Trust in God

1. Psalm 23	"Though I pass through a gloomy valley, I fear no harm."
2. Psalm 27	"Yahweh is the fortress of my life; of whom should I be afraid?"
3. Luke 7:1–10	"Not even in Israel have I found faith like this."
4. Matthew 6:25–34	"Do not worry about tomorrow. Tomorrow will take care of itself."

5. John 14:1–2   "Do not let your hearts be troubled."
6. Mark 4:35–41   "Why are you so terrified? How is it that you have no faith?"
7. Mark 5:35–43   "Do not be afraid: only have faith."

Forgiveness
1. Matthew 9:9–13   "I did not come to call the virtuous, but sinners."
2. Luke 7:36–50   "It is the man who is forgiven little who shows little love."
3. John 8:1–11   "If there is one of you who has not sinned, let him be the first to throw a stone at her."
4. Luke 15:1–7   "There will be more joy in heaven over one repentant sinner than over ninety-nine virtuous men who have no need of repentance."
5. Matthew 18:21–22   "Lord, how often must I forgive my brother if he wrongs me?"
6. Colossians 3:12–15   "May the peace of Christ reign in your hearts."
7. John 20:19–23   "Peace be with you."

Love in Action
1. Matthew 5:43–48   "Love your enemies and pray for those who persecute you."
2. Luke 6:36–37   "Be compassionate as your Father is compassionate."
3. Mark 12:28–34   "You must love your neighbor as yourself."
4. John 15:9–13   "This is my commandment: love one another."

5. Luke 10:25–37   "Which of these three do you think proved himself to be a neighbor to the man?"

6. 1 John 4:7–8   "God is love."

7. 1 Corinthians 13: 1–7 "If I have all the eloquence of men or of angels, but speak without love, I am simply a gong booming or a cymbal clashing."

Prayer

1. Psalm 63   "God, you are my God. I am seeking you."

2. Psalm 42:2–3   "As a doe longs for running streams, so my soul longs for you, my God."

3. Matthew 6:5–15   "Our Father in heaven, may your name be held holy."

4. Matthew 7:7–11   "Ask, and it will be given to you; search, and you will find."

5. Luke 18:9–14   "God, be merciful to me, a sinner."

6. 1 Thessalonians 5: 16–18   "Pray constantly."

7. Ephesians 1:15–19   "May the God of our Lord Jesus Christ give you a spirit of wisdom and perception."

The Path to Holiness

1. Psalm 1   "Happy the man . . . who finds his pleasure in the law of Yahweh."

2. Mark 8:34–37   "Anyone who wants to save his life will lose it."

3. Matthew 5:1–12   "Happy those who hunger and thirst for what is right."

4. Philippians 3:7–16   "I am still running trying to capture the prize for which Christ Jesus captured me."

5. John 12:24–25   "Unless a grain of wheat falls on the ground and dies, it remains but a grain."

6. Colossians 3:1–10   "The life you have is hidden with Christ in God."

7. Matthew 25:31–36   "Insofar as you did this to one of the least of these brothers of mine, you did it to me."